FROM THE CLIFFS OF CORNWALL TO KILIMANJARO

THE TREKKER'S TALE

ERIC MARKS

Copyright © 2022 Eric Marks

The moral right of the author has been asserted.

Apart from any fair dealing for the purposes of research or private study, or criticism or review, as permitted under the Copyright, Designs and Patents Act 1988, this publication may only be reproduced, stored or transmitted, in any form or by any means, with the prior permission in writing of the publishers, or in the case of reprographic reproduction in accordance with the terms of licences issued by the Copyright Licensing Agency. Enquiries concerning reproduction outside those terms should be sent to the publishers.

Matador
Unit E2 Airfield Business Park,
Harrison Road, Market Harborough,
Leicestershire. LE16 7UL
Tel: 0116 2792299
Email: books@troubador.co.uk
Web: www.troubador.co.uk/matador
Twitter: @matadorbooks

ISBN 978 1803131 382

British Library Cataloguing in Publication Data.
A catalogue record for this book is available from the British Library.

Printed and bound by CPI Group (UK) Ltd, Croydon, CR0 4YY
Typeset in 11pt Minion Pro by Troubador Publishing Ltd, Leicester, UK

Matador is an imprint of Troubador Publishing Ltd

FROM THE CLIFFS
OF CORNWALL TO
KILIMANJARO

I dedicate this book to my nephew, friend, and outstanding trekking companion, Jonathan Starkey Kennedy (Jon).

We thought that we knew each other pretty well, but unexpected strengths and weaknesses emerged during our training and mountain trekking. These only served to deepen our mutual respect, and I am happy to say that we are still on very good terms.

As you will see, our whole adventure was exciting, gruelling, spellbinding, and humbling. It was also interspersed with strange and exhilarating events, and even stranger people we met along the way. But my wicked sense of humour –usually at Jon's expense –punctuated the story.

Jon, you put up with all this from me so well that I take immense pleasure in dedicating this book to you. No one could wish for a better friend and walking companion.

With heartfelt thanks and great respect,
Eric

ONE

I didn't know what a life-focusing event I was letting myself in for at the dinner that evening. You may have experienced something similar. You listen, captivated, to a friend talking enthusiastically about some upcoming event that has the lure of adventure about it. Then, out of the blue, you are invited to join your friend on the trip of a lifetime. You hesitate, but after a couple of glasses of good wine, you know that this is an irresistible force. I hesitated for a while longer in order to give the impression that I was a carefully reasoning sort of guy. But I knew that I was hooked. My life had changed to a different level, to a different tempo. What a strange thing to have happened in my seventy-sixth year! In my mind I was still in my early twenties, just as well when I reflected on what lay ahead of me.

The friend in this case was my nephew, Jonathan. He wanted desperately to climb a substantial mountain, and Kilimanjaro in Tanzania was his choice. He had no idea just how difficult it would be to get a climbing buddy, and after exhausting his lists of 'probables and possibles', he unleashed his persuasive magic on me... a last resort.

But first, let me tell you something about ourselves before we all set out together on what was to be quite an adventure. This adventure I will never forget, not only because it turned out to be so exhilarating but also because it was stunningly different from what I expected it to be.

My nephew Jonathan was forty-eight and very keen on staying fit and healthy. He worked out regularly in his local gym but lived in a part of the country that is lacking in hills; in fact, it is pancake-flat. Clearly, this was not ideal training ground for big hills and mountains. Being in a quite high position in the Metropolitan Police, he was a resourceful guy. He travelled down from London, to where I live in Plymouth, for training on the steep ground of Dartmoor and, of course, on the South West Coast Path for its frequently steep and testing terrain. Another incentive for travelling down to visit my wife, Judith, and me is that we always fed him well. His mother, Vivien – Judith's sister – also lives in Plymouth. She provided him with accommodation and also fed him well to keep his strength up!

Jonathan lives for sport of all types, and indeed it could be said that sport is his life, next to his wife and four daughters. Jon (as he prefers to be called) had picked up several sports injuries in his career. These would need to be treated with great care in the course of our training and the Kilimanjaro expedition itself. It was these injuries that would possibly give me a chance to keep up to his pace over the many trials ahead of us; time would tell.

Jon is quite tall, good-looking in a rugged, outdoor way, and has a powerful build. He has even less hair than I have, and that is saying something, believe me. His favourite clothing is shorts and T-shirt, but this may not have been viable on the heights of Kilimanjaro after the first day or two. Jon loves to talk with people we meet when we are out walking. Often within seconds he has them believing that he is my carer and that I am on day release. It's amazing how many people accept what he says, even when I tell them that he is telling 'porkies'.

As regards his general effect upon me, let me say right here at the outset that I have the highest regard for Jon. He is inspirational.

He is also reliable, especially in an emergency. His long years in the police have helped to shape him into someone special. He is intelligent and knowledgeable, just the sort of guy to have with you if things take a turn for the worse. Jon is a great non-fiction reader with wide-ranging knowledge. A possible downside is that he doesn't always suffer fools gladly. Clearly, I would need to be careful in what I said and did.

So, what about me? What can I tell you that will help to illuminate the events that are about to unfold?

Having left the Royal Marines in 1969, I had kept myself reasonably fit. This had been achieved mainly by regular walking with our various Labradors over the years and occasional two-day backpacking trips. But all that changed when, at the age of seventy-two, I joined my local gym. I had gradually become aware that my level of activity was not adequate to keep me in good condition for my later years. Something had to be done, and fast, because the body keeps a careful reckoning.

Joining the gym was a revelation to me. The high-tech nature of the gym equipment was far removed from what I remembered about my days in the armed services.

In those days there were wall bars, vaulting horses, medicine balls, skipping ropes, climbing ropes, and not much else. That being said, the assault courses and endurance marches on Dartmoor more than made up for the lack of gym equipment.

I engaged with much of the new fitness gear and machines in the local gym, and within a few months I became fitter and stronger. Little did I know at that time just how essential all this was to become in three years' time when Jon invited me to join him on this African adventure. But first, let me tell you some more about the two of us and about our similarities and striking differences. This was to become important over our months of training and on the expedition itself.

Jon enjoys fine food and wine, whereas I have little interest in food other than as fuel for my active life, although I do enjoy a glass of wine. I love the stoical lot of the backpacker, walking alone, carrying everything I need for a few days of camping. The feeling of self-sufficiency gives me a real buzz. Jon, on the other hand, detests camping. I am sure that he would also decline the alfresco food I would serve up to him at the end of a hard day's backpacking.

I also am a keen reader but generally in literature and philosophy. Jon loves the modern popular music scene, whereas I am steeped in classical music from the Renaissance to the present time.

When it comes to walking interests, Jon is mainly in love with the lure of the big mountains. I am much more enamoured with distance-walking over attractive, but often challenging, countryside. As you can appreciate, I was stepping outside my comfort zone when it came to our expedition to Mount Kilimanjaro. Having said that, Jon was also stepping outside his comfort zone and into a nightmare, as the route he eventually decided on involved several days of camping. This wasn't spotted at the outset when Jon booked the trip – glad it wasn't me!

* * *

Now, let's talk commitment. Let's *go for it* as we were summoned to do on some of the premium-priced sports gear. Yes! It was time to select a specialist travel company, book the expedition, and pay our deposits in resolute style. I hope you are adventure-ready for what was about to happen over the months of training that lay ahead and then the trip of a lifetime to Africa and the great Kilimanjaro volcano. Now, let's go forward, because I cannot wait to tell you this story. See you in chapter two.

TWO

The irresistible urge to book for the expedition overtook my natural curiosity to know exactly what I was getting into. Yes, I blundered into this one. Jon knew a little about Kilimanjaro, but in the event, this was only a starting point. We both had a lot to learn.

Our learning process really started with the arrival of the travel brochure. This was glossy, sparkling, glistening, and crammed with a feast of photographs showing what awaited us. If we thought we were keen to go before sending for the brochure and paying our deposits, now we were buzzing with anticipation. We had forgotten conveniently that this was only March 2018, and we had to wait until September before flying out to Africa. Not only that, but first we had five months of intensive training in front of us. But before planning our training in detail, we needed to find out much more about that mountain and what it would demand of us. The more we delved into the Kilimanjaro story, the more gripping it became. What follows in this chapter is the fruit of that startling research.

* * *

Kilimanjaro is the highest mountain in Africa and one of the Seven Summits challenge to climb the highest mountain in each of the world's seven continents. Kilimanjaro, like many mountains, is a killer in more senses than one! Standing at 5895 metres above sea level, it is roughly two-thirds the height of Everest. Some authorities take the view that it is somewhere between five hundred thousand and 750,000 years old and that it erupted out of the earth during the time when the Great Rift Valley was formed.

This mountain is a dormant volcano. In fact, it is the highest free-standing volcano in the world. Free-standing in this sense means that it is not in a mountain range with other mountains alongside it but geologically completely alone in its grandeur. When one first sees 'Kili' rising from the relatively flat terrain around it, you can probably imagine some of the effect on the senses. Awe-inspiring comes close but not close enough to really describe the excitement if you are just on the point of trekking to its summit. That is a feeling beyond my ability to convey.

The mountain lies approximately three degrees south of the equator. This has some bearing on the stars to be seen in the night sky, but more of that later. The position in terms of the equator gives Tanzania a weather pattern that needs to be taken fully into account when planning an expedition to Kilimanjaro. We went in early September, and the weather was excellent. October's weather is also generally very good, but some months can be less favourable or even dire.

Kilimanjaro has three major volcanic cones. The main cone is Kibo, and this is right on top of the mountain. Mawenzi is lower down and is classed as being extinct. Shira is also classed as extinct. But Kibo is merely dormant. Some scientists in recent years have detected signs that Kibo could erupt again. In fact, the seething magma is thought to be no more than half a kilometre below the surface of the main cone's ash pit in the Reusch Crater, and it could even be shallower than that. You would feel the heat coming up through the ground in that crater. You would also smell the sulphur dioxide percolating up through the ash. I will tell you a deeply sad story about the other main cone, Mawenzi, later on in this account of our expedition.

How ferocious a killer is Kilimanjaro? This is a hard question to answer, but there are some indications. The figures suggest that there could be an average of ten to thirty deaths a year on the mountain. Accuracy is not possible because official figures are notoriously difficult to come by. This mountain is an important economic resource, especially in such a relatively poor country. However, the likely main cause of death is probably due to the effects of serious altitude sickness. It appears that about a thousand trekkers on average every year have to be evacuated from Kilimanjaro. Most of these people are suffering from the more serious effects of altitude sickness.

This sickness is not a subject to treat lightly. Many trekkers on this mountain suffer from the effects of altitude. But when the effects progress beyond a certain level, this must be brought to the attention of the group leader who will know whether evacuation is necessary. The trekking guides are highly experienced, yet even they cannot always detect the danger signs. They will explain the different levels of altitude sickness to you very carefully at the beginning of the expedition. Your responsibility is to keep them fully informed if you find yourself deteriorating from the initial effects into something more serious and dangerous.

To give you some idea of the size of Kilimanjaro, its base covers roughly the same area as the county of Cornwall in the United Kingdom. That area is 1,376 square miles, or 3,563 square kilometres. It is massive!

There are four main routes up this mountain. The most used route is the Marangu, often playfully called the 'Coca-Cola Route', and it approaches the mountain from the south. This is the route that offers basic hut accommodation instead of the usual camping. Sleeping in the huts leaves the trekker open to multiple snoring probabilities from the other inmates, but at least you do not have to sleep on the cold ground with only a thin insulating mat and the sleeping bag between you and the rough terrain under the tent.

A popular and well-used route is Lemosho. This one comes onto the mountain from a westerly direction. A useful feature of this route is that an extra day can sometimes be booked, and this would make it a seven-day stretch rather than the typical six days. That extra day gives the trekker a better chance of coping with the altitude and also gives a better chance of reaching the summit or reaching it without so much suffering… yes! Suffering… all will be revealed shortly.

The Rongai route approaches the mountain from the northeast, from a starting point very close to the Kenyan border with Tanzania. It is quite different from the other routes in that it hasn't any real rainforest to speak of, and the terrain as you gradually trek up the mountain is relatively arid. Water can also be a problem outside the rainy season. More porters will be needed to carry sufficient water in the drier months of the year. The bonus is that there may be more chance of seeing wildlife on this route. In any event, it has become more popular in recent years, even though it takes longer to travel to the starting point.

Jon had earlier researched the different routes and the typical costs of each one. He recommended the route not touched on yet, and this is the Machame route (the 'ch' is pronounced usually as 'sh').

The Machame route is often regarded as the most demanding in terms of steepness. But it wins out for its scenic beauty. The route involves camping all the way up and down the mountain, so I was surprised that Jon, with his aversion to camping, didn't choose the 'Coca-Cola Route' with the hut accommodation. That being said, Jon did get us a good deal from the organising company, and the availability of huts was not apparent at the time of booking.

With all this information, Jon and I could start planning our training. Multi-day backpacking had been highly recommended. Leg-strengthening work in the gym, as well as general fitness training, had also been advised. So, this is where the rubber hits the road! But first, in order to find out how other trekkers fared, and how their experiences could help us draw up our training plan, I read a few books by some of those trekkers. There is also a great deal of information on YouTube in some impressive films.

THREE

The books I read about Kilimanjaro expeditions all screamed out the shocking fact that this mountain takes no prisoners. The final ascent to the summit can be, for most people, a real nightmare. Imagine struggling up a steep slope of very fine, loose volcanic cinders or scree. Then picture the frustration of taking a demanding step upwards, only to feel your boots slipping back part of the length of that forward pace. Another problem is that you have to negotiate many boulders en route. This goes on for several gruelling hours. Even worse than all that, the ascent to the summit takes place at night, and unless you are lucky, it will be mercilessly cold. In fact, it could be the coldest night of your life. Add to this that you are up against this climb after a hard day's trekking, followed by a meal and only about three hours of rest before setting off at midnight, and you get some idea of the challenges just waiting for you in the illuminated world of your headlamp's beam.

The terrain for the whole trek up this mountain is changeable and challenging in its own special way. When you also factor in the ever-changing weather, you can appreciate why this monster of Kilimanjaro is called the chameleon mountain. A writer in one of the books I read emphasised that dangers were lurking all around with every step. While that way of putting it wasn't featured in such a dramatic way in any of the other books I read about this mountain, it seems to me in retrospect that this guy was not far from the truth, starting from at least the third day of the ascent.

Allied to the dangers on the mountain, there are also the not-uncommon dangers of enemies to one's health lurking in these parts of Africa. Ebola and severe gastroenteritis are threats to be aware of. But these dangers should be taken in perspective, as you would have to be really unlucky to contract anything on that scale.

Some accounts of the trek up Kilimanjaro describe the rain and cold in the lower reaches of the mountain at certain times of the year. Add these to what could be an exhausted state at the end of a long trek up the steep slopes, and you will understand how a feeling of despondency may set in. You may also be cold and hungry while you wait for the support team to get the meal under way. The warmth of the dining tent will then wrap you in ecstasy when you finally get the call to dinner. Yes, the rain can be a problem at certain times of the year. The best approach is to check carefully with your tour organiser for the more comfortable months to choose. I am told that late December is very popular when you tackle the final ascent to the summit so that you arrive at the top on New Year's Day. But December can be quite a wet and cold month, with all that that entails. In any event, the popularity of that time of year cannot be denied.

One thing kept being mentioned in the accounts I read about other people's experiences on the mountain. Muscle aches, leg joint pains, headaches, and a gradual feeling of exhaustion were the most prominent, along with the increasing problem of oxygen depletion as the trekkers climbed higher. The absence of any in-depth detail on their training methods was particularly exasperating because it could have given us something to figure into our own training plan.

Another feature of the books I studied was the general tendency of most writers to keep asking themselves the big question: *why am I doing this?* This also seems to be a question that even very experienced climbers and trekkers ask themselves in at least the early stages of big expeditions. One useful piece of advice I read somewhere is to sit down quietly and reflect on at least the three biggest reasons you are going to do whatever it is you are committing to. This clearly can be used in various contexts, not just for expeditions.

Yet another crushing feature that was often spoken of was the problem with sleeping. This was partly due to the cold. Another factor was the quite rough ground that was unavoidably used for the campsites. Speaking from personal experience, I suspect that for most people, it takes a few days' adjustment to feel comfortable enough to get a really good night's sleep in a sleeping bag on cold and hard ground and in a cold tent. The demands that this mountain puts on the body and mind are made even harder without a proper night's rest. This is even more critical if every night is a tossing and turning marathon of restlessness. Anyone who has mastered long-duration levitation for several hours at a time has a decided advantage when it comes to sleeping on rough terrain.

The strong wind can also be a real problem. It can give the feeling that it is cutting right into the marrow of your bones. Just imagine what this will be like if you are unfortunate enough to get caught in a blizzard on the higher reaches of the mountain! And this can happen. A quilted jacket designed for such mountain conditions is definitely recommended. Tinted snow glasses of good quality should also be on your kit list. The glare from the sunlight reflected off snow and ice in the glacier region at the summit can be extremely hard on the eyes. And if you are caught in a snowstorm, well…

So, there is the risk of nausea, throbbing headaches, dizziness, seriously aching leg muscles, aching joints. Add in the probable need to stop and struggle for breath every hundred steps or so, and you can appreciate that getting to the summit in the later stages of the expedition is by no means a done deal. This will be confirmed dramatically when you struggle past trekkers of all ages who are all in and where the guides are arranging for evacuations before they have a real emergency on their hands. Ponder also on the top-flight sportspeople who have not been able to get to the summit. Fitness is vital for this ascent, but the effect of altitude can affect anyone regardless of their physical preparedness or age. That is an aspect that is not, apparently, something you can prepare for if you live in a country like the UK and cannot get access to high-altitude training. Whether you can get to the summit of Kilimanjaro, or any other big trekking mountain, will be down to your physical and mental resources but especially to the way your body can cope with altitude.

These accounts that I had been studying all pointed to the fact that Jon and I would be digging deep into our physical and mental reserves to reach the summit. In any event, we were committed now and would just have to make the best of it. Furthermore, this foretaste of what lay in store for us could not even offer encouragement for the descent from the summit. This would be another stern test but a contrasting one.

Many walkers find that coming downhill can be just as arduous as the ascent. This is where your boots need to be fitted properly. The one thing you don't want is your feet sliding forward with your toes banging into the boots' toecap area. Bruised toenails will obviously be painful, and they will probably lift away from the toe. It could be months before the nails come completely away as new nails develop. So, first of all, it pays to buy boots that are not too small or too narrow. Small boots will increase the chance of your toes hammering into the hard resistance of the toecap. Boots that are too roomy in length will allow free movement of the feet to set up friction as you walk and could still slide forward enough to cause toenail bashing.

The answer is to try a range of boots in an outdoor shop in light of what I described. Some specialist outdoor shops will be able to offer a welcome fitting service, and this is what I would always try to get. Another answer is to have the boots handmade, but be prepared to pay a lot more for them. Once you have a well-fitting pair of rough terrain boots, the other important part is to tie the laces in such a way that your feet are held securely but comfortably in the area of the instep in order to minimise any sliding of the feet. It is well worth the effort to achieve this.

Now, back to the descent from the summit of Kilimanjaro. The lava scree encountered on the ascent will now present you with the opposite problem; you will find yourself sliding forwards and not backwards. The time factor also comes into this as you need to be down to the final camp before darkness wraps itself around the tricky route ahead.

Scree running is encouraged at this point in order to keep up to schedule. It can be dangerous if you are not careful. The technique seems simple enough. You set off from the top of a scree slope at a jogging pace, or maybe a bit faster. The secret is to just relax carefully into the steep, downwards slope and follow the advice of your guides and porters. They will show you how it is done. The pace will probably increase as your confidence rises. At a certain speed, your boots act like skies, so it is important to keep watching out for rocks ahead of you and take evasive action in plenty of time.

Not everyone will find this easy. The porters will be keeping a watch on each person's progress and will help out where necessary. This can result in you having two porters grabbing an elbow each, instructing you to keep your feet clear of the scree, and whisking you down – quite exhilarating! Accidents do sometimes happen during the scree running, and out of nowhere, it seems, a stretcher is produced to get the casualty down to the overnight camp and any medical attention that may be needed.

Taking all of this detail to heart, the next phase facing Jon and I was to draw up a serious training plan and to schedule it to cover the five months remaining before we set off. Our excitement was undiminished, yet an undercurrent of trepidation was there as well.

How should we structure our training? What training could we do together, and what would need to be done apart? My training time was relatively easy to fit in, but Jon had more commitments to figure into our plan. How would all this pan out? Read all about it in the next chapter, the last one before the rubber hits the ground running.

FOUR

So, here we are at the planning stage. This plan had to be good in light of what I had distilled from the experiences of several other struggling Kilimanjaro trekkers. Our training advice from the expedition company, with whom we had booked, put emphasis on multi-day backpacking or trekking over demanding terrain. The South West Coast Path around the north coast of Somerset, Devon, and Cornwall offered this in lavish quantities, so we decided on a trek from Minehead in Somerset to Penzance in Cornwall.

I had trekked and wild camped some of this route before, but this time we would not be carrying a tent, cooking gear, or quantities of food to last for a few days, much to Jon's relief. Large daypacks would suffice, as we would be staying in prearranged accommodation. Nevertheless, there were many, many hills and cliffs waiting to test us in gruelling ways throughout the 273 miles.

Walking this coastal path is a memorable experience and often breathtaking in more ways than one! The whole route from Minehead to Poole in Dorset is 630 miles long over strikingly varied terrain. Much of it is like a rollercoaster. You struggle up a steep and endless cliff path and welcome the thought of the downhill part that often comes next. But then the legs and knees can object in different ways than they did on the upwards journey. At the same time, you know that downhill sections come with the promise of yet another uphill challenge, and so each day progresses until the next overnight stop is reached. You are probably getting the impression that this has the potential to be excellent training ground. I will share that experience with you in some detail as we tackle this monster during May, June, and July of 2018, our Kilimanjaro year.

Other commitments would make it difficult to tackle the complete route from Minehead to Penzance in one hit, so we agreed to split the journey into three parts. Part one would be from Minehead to Barnstaple. This distance is almost seventy miles over some good training ground.

The second phase of the journey would be from Barnstaple to Newquay in Cornwall. This 120-mile section is even more demanding, with some particularly big cliff climbs. I had in the past trekked the whole of this section, so I knew what to expect. I thought it better not to describe it in too much detail to Jon. Some unforgettable things happened to me on that previous trek about forty years ago, and I will tell you all about them as our trek gets under way.

The final part of the journey would be from Newquay to Penzance in Cornwall, a distance of eighty-three miles. This includes some of the most scenic and wild terrain of the entire route, and I have in the past trekked about half of this epic journey. Again, I have had some memorable experiences on this section of our utterly unique coastal footpath, and I look forward to telling you about them as the journey unfolds.

I should tell you that arranging the logistics for these three training trips will not always be easy or straightforward. But you may find many of the travel details helpful if you are tempted to try some of these walks yourself. For us – travelling from Plymouth on the southern side of Devon – the railway service was going to be by far the easiest to arrange. Jon is well-versed in logistics, so he volunteered to sort this out while I planned the walking sections for each day.

To get to Minehead from Plymouth, the train service is fast and frequent to the town of Taunton in central Somerset. From Taunton there is a good bus service to Minehead where we will start the big journey. I haven't told Jon at this stage, but whenever we need to catch a bus, he will have to pay, but I get free bus travel by just showing my free senior citizen's bus pass. Jon will be theatrically incensed, especially if we need to travel on several buses during the course of our travels, but I will try my hardest not to gloat (at least not openly).

Breaking the first section of our journey at Barnstaple in north Devon will allow us to pick up a branch line train to Exeter in Devon where we can then get a main-line train back to Plymouth. So that will complete the May part of the trek training, and we have allowed four days to complete it.

In June we will travel by train back to Barnstaple to start the second leg of the journey. This involves changing trains at Exeter from the main-line service to a branch line for the connection to Barnstaple. The first leg of this walking route will take us to Bideford, and then on to Newquay in Cornwall. From Newquay we will take the direct train back to Plymouth.

In July we will travel back to Newquay to start the final part of the eighty-three-mile walk to Penzance. The rail service from Penzance back to Plymouth is good, so the basic logistics seem to be in place, but as we all know, life can be full of surprises.

* * *

Now we come to the fun bit! This is where we tried to arrange reasonably priced accommodation that would fit in conveniently with the end of each day's training walk.

Jon took over this task, and I didn't envy him. We realised that much of the accommodation on offer was highly priced and in the wrong place for us. This was because our proposed daily training mileage didn't fit conveniently into those places where reasonably priced accommodation could be found easily. This left Jon with the choice between youth hostels and Airbnbs. He didn't seem to be keen on hostels, but over certain sections of the route, hostels appeared to be our best (and sometimes only) bet. Little did we know what lay in store for us at these hostels; all will be revealed to you in due course.

Upon further consideration, we found that we only needed four Airbnbs for the entire trip. I arranged our first overnight stay at an attractive farmhouse where I had stayed several times before in the village of Porlock. This was just at the right distance from our starting point of Minehead and was perfect for the short first day of walking after travelling to Minehead from Plymouth by train. There would be the added attraction of an excellent breakfast prepared by our host David. Another great advantage was being able to visit the Ship Inn, just a short distance from David's farmhouse.

The Ship Inn is steeped in history and may have been the place where the poet Samuel Taylor Coleridge wrote his famous poem *Kubla Khan*, although there are other strong claims from locations within a short distance of Porlock where the poem could have been written. But more of Porlock when we reach the village, once we start the eagerly anticipated walk.

I arranged the hostel accommodation, and there were seven of them altogether. Add in the other accommodations and we arrive at the grand total of twelve overnight stops. Each one had its own peculiarities, as you will find out when we experience them en route.

* * *

Now, let me throw a spanner in the works! There was by this time a growing interest in my local gym about our planned training exploits. In fact, I had planned to do an extra training walk by myself in April while Jon was finishing off his time in the Metropolitan Police. Although part of the walk with Jon in July would involve the route between St Ives in Cornwall to Penzance, I decided on that same route for my extra training in April. That walk is a particular favourite of mine, and I hadn't walked it for at least three years. This was a wonderful idea, and it was only partially worrying because of the amount of rainfall we had been experiencing during the previous months of winter. There had been a lot of it, and here we were in mid-March with the rain still reluctant to let the warm sunshine of spring have more than a teasing chance to raise everyone's spirits. As incredulous as this may sound to you, six of my friends at the gym pressed me to open up the two-day walk to them as well. I tried to alert them to the probability of some lingering and deep mud on the coastal footpath, and the possibility of the rainy weather continuing, but this didn't seem to be important to them. It was agreed that we would all go on this walk together. There were to be seven of us, so the obvious way to think of ourselves was The Magnificent Seven – yeah, OK!

FIVE

The day arrived for the seven of us to set off for St Ives in Cornwall. My friend Dave was going to drive three of us down to our starting (and finishing) point at Penzance, and Karen, his wife was going to drive two of the others down in her car. The seventh member of our group, Brian, was already down at St Ives and would meet us when we arrived there. It was Brian's wedding anniversary on the second day of our walk, and his wife would be waiting for him when we arrived back in Penzance after the two days of hard walking that lay in store for us. The plan was for Brian and his wife to have a special celebration meal in a lovely hotel in Penzance, stay the night, and travel back to Plymouth the day after. But the best laid plans… more of that later.

In order to get to St Ives, have breakfast, and hit the trail by about 8.30am, we needed to leave Plymouth at 5am. My alarm clock shot a malicious jolt into my sleeping brain at 4am. How my wife Judith could sleep through that I do not know. Now fully awake, I shaved, did a few stretches to fire up my system, got the coffee under way, and did a last-minute check through my packing list. I took a thoughtful cup of tea in to Judith, who managed to give me a disoriented thank you.

Dave arrived just before 5am. We loaded up the car and set off to pick up Arthur. He lived about three miles away on our planned route. Just as we left my house, the rain started and splattered noisily on the windscreen. It was so noisy and vicious because there was hail mixed in with the rain. Have you ever had that sinking feeling when your worst fears about the weather are being worked out in front you? This sinking feeling can be acute when you are just setting out on an endurance walking trip. What in heaven's name will the next two days lavish upon us?

Arthur was waiting for us at the appointed place. He is the second eldest in our group, and I am the eldest. He is a veteran trekker and has been on expeditions to countless exotic locations around the world over many years. Each one of us in our walking group has plenty of trekking experience, but Arthur is right out in front with his exploits. I have encouraged him to write a book about his travels as it would be most interesting.

The rain stopped. With crossed fingers for good weather, we drove on into the blackness of the pre-dawn. The journey to Penzance should take two hours, especially on the virtually deserted road. Headlights appeared behind us, and Dave's wife Karen overtook us. Dave put on a show of indignation and gave a rude gesture as Karen's two passengers, Pearl and Richard, joyfully waved just as Karen's car launched a tumult of road spray across our windscreen.

We drove on in convoy for another hour or so into the reluctant dawn. Then, just as a miserable patch of brass-coloured clouds sulked through in the east, the rain sliced down again.

* * *

Penzance was not looking its usual jaunty self. The sky was leaden. This could be a fine day for a Cornish funeral with such a backdrop. We found the extra-long-stay car park without any difficulty and paid for two full days' parking to help swell the local council's bulging coffers.

The town was beginning to wake up, but the weather had seemingly affected everything and everybody. As I was thinking this, the sky brightened a little, then a little bit more; then a shaft of sunlight beamed onto our disbelieving faces. I almost morphed into my yoga 'salute to the sun' exercises, but Karen, Pearl, and Richard walked over to join the three of us and I joined in the joyous greetings to start our day off. We couldn't quite accept the change in the weather, but it was definitely happening; this surprise sunshine, in spite of our previous collective pessimism, revived our spirits no end. What a wonderful thing human adaptability is!

It had been my job to prearrange the minibus to take us from Penzance to St Ives. I telephoned the taxi company, and it was confirmed that we would be picked up in about five minutes. The minibus arrived very quickly, and I breathed a sigh of relief. Having arranged this several weeks earlier, and being assured that everything had been booked in, I was surprised to learn only three days ago, when I rang to do a last-minute check, that everything depended on the driver not being called away to do any urgent school runs for the education authority at short notice! We all breathed a sigh of relief. The bus service to St Ives did not start at that time of year until about 8.30am, the same time we had planned to set out on the walk from St Ives, after having joined up with Brian and had a good breakfast together.

The minibus took us on a quiet road to St Ives, and we arrived at 7.30am in plenty of time. We spotted a Wetherspoon restaurant in the town that opened at 8am. This seemed ideal for our breakfast stop, and we were sure that Brian would spot us if we all sat in the front window seat. The breakfast set us up well for the walk ahead and proved to be excellent value for money. Brian spotted us and joined the merry band. As we were leaving the restaurant, I happened to spot a notice stating that beer was not being sold until 9am. Why the first hour of trading was 'dry' is a mystery, probably something to do with planning laws.

Daypacks were hoisted onto backs, and off we set through the town and down to the harbour area. St Ives is world famous among artists for its quality of light. Its clarity and ability to bring out the sumptuous colours of this atmospheric old town is what painters dream of. Many famous artists have travelled to this place for the subjects it offers them, and many have made St Ives their home. This morning with the sun warming us, the seagulls swooping and shrieking out, the smell of freshly caught fish being unloaded from the small boats, and the town waking up to another day in this glorious spot sent our spirits bounding.

We took some photographs as we wended our way along the harbour front, and I found myself wishing that I could have been a good painter instead of just another dauber. But photography is still painting with light, so I will be thankful for small mercies because people seem to enjoy looking at my photographs, and I enjoy taking them. In any event, we approached the end of the harbour and then saw the wonderful surfing beach of Porthmeor; what a lovely old Cornish name!

We saw two intrepid surfers striding out early towards the empty lines of surf patterning out from the glittering sand. Further out was a small fishing boat lolling lazily with the gentle swell waves. And the sun was still shining and warming everything. Was winter really over? We could but hope.

As we passed the wonderfully positioned Tate St Ives art gallery, I looked across into the distance at the real start of our first day's walk. The first section of that beckoning coastline looked marvellous in that exciting moment, and it brought back distant memories of the first time I walked this way.

* * *

It was in the early 1970s that I felt a yearning to buy some good backpacking gear and explore the Cornish coastal footpath. It was that lovely time between the end of spring and the beginning of summer when I drove down to Penzance to start what would become an unforgettable adventure.

Car parking at that time was as easy as just finding a sensible space and leaving the car there until the evening of the following day at the end of the walk. There wasn't any charge, and there were very few double yellow lines in those days. How much simpler and easier everything seemed in those far-off days!

I found the bus for St Ives as it was just leaving the bus station and clambered aboard. The driver was pleasant and helpful, and that early morning bus journey in the sunshine got me in the right mood for what followed.

I had never been to St Ives before, and the effect that the town and seascape had on me was beyond anything I could have imagined. The glowing light, the tropical blue-green of the sea, the salty smells of the fish and the harbour carried on the gentle breezes of the early morning, all melded into an intoxicating atmosphere of expectancy. The memory of this day would live with me for the rest of my life, and if it was to be my final thought, what a way to sum up my very best experiences here on earth! Looking back on that morning now, I can see just what a precious jewel of memory it became for me.

That impression, as deep and glorious as it had been, set the scene for what happened next. The back lane I was following through the town suddenly opened out into my first view of Porthmeor Beach. I don't think it had become a surfing Mecca in those days; in any event, the beach happened to be empty of activity on this perfect morning, apart from two bass anglers hoping to strike it lucky by casting out just beyond the third breaker line. This is often the classic area to intercept fish feeding on marine life scoured out by the undertow from the sandy shallows. But as stunning as the beach scene was, the view towards the start of the coastal footpath, and the seascape shimmering beyond, left me overwhelmed with expectation.

I quickly walked the final few hundred yards to the beginning of the path. Here I was at the start of what would become my great backpacking passion up to the present day. The sun had already given a strong hint that this day was going to be a hot one. I took off my backpack, shed my lightweight jacket, took a long drink of water, and set off on the pathway walking on air, even with the heavy pack strapped again to my back.

After a few minutes, the path took me close to a small rocky outcrop. I walked out onto the rock platform to gaze down into the deep water. The gentle swell curves glistened in the sunlight. As I looked down, the long fronds of kelp swayed and waved in time to the languorous swell. It had never occurred to me before, but such animation in the sea is like the ocean's pulse.

I started walking again after that brief detour and almost at once faced a choice of paths to follow. The upper path seemed more directly forward, if rather steeper than the lower one. The upper path won, and off I went.

A minute or two into the steady climb took me to a short section of blackthorn hedge in delightful bloom. Gorse had also blended itself like a tapestry into the hedge, and its sun-yellow flowers complemented the glory of this gentle spring morning. The fragrance of the gorse flowers floated out into the world, already overbrimming with such heady sensuousness. I had never experienced such pleasure in nature before.

Then, just to underline the specialness of this day, I heard the most exquisite birdsong coming from the hedge within just a few feet of me. There on a branch sat a song thrush. I think it was singing for pure joy because it felt the same way about this special morning as I did. This troubadour gazed straight at me as it sang, almost as if it wanted to serenade me. I can still feel the thrill of that moment nearly fifty years on.

It must have been several years later that I came across two comments in my reading that let me appreciate even more what I had experienced that morning. The first piece was about a starling in a cage in a Viennese shop. Its song was so lyrical that a customer in the shop just had to buy it and take it home to care for it. Apparently, this bird inspired some sublime music in its owner's compositions; the owner's name? Mozart.

The second piece concerned something that was attributed to Richard Strauss's librettist, Hugo von Hofmannsthal. He said that we find reality and our true selves in the moments of our greatest enchantment. That morning, with the birdsong, and the way my spirits were lifted by the gentle weather, the sunlight, the murmuring sea, and the tingling anticipation of what else lay ahead for me that remarkable day, truly were some of my greatest moments of enchantment.

You can probably imagine how difficult it was to leave this spot of my epiphany. Yes, it was an epiphany, one that has stayed with me over the many years since that day. Backpacking had now become one of the most important things in my life.

* * *

The sun grew even warmer as I climbed to the top of the slope. Rough ground now became a regular feature of the pathway, but apart from occasional springs and rivulets, the ground was dry. I had started to drink more frequently, and niggling thoughts started to intrude about where I might get a refill for the two-litre water bottle. Although it is tempting to risk taking drinking water from the streams and brooks en route, the consequences could be dire. It was fortunate that I had some water purification tablets in my first aid kit, but with luck I might be able avoid having to use these things with their unpleasant taste.

I checked the map for any likely looking places where water might be available, but the map didn't offer any encouragement. St Just looked favourable, but it happened to be right at the end of this first day's trek. The sun's heat rippled down without any sign of a let-up, so water consumption had to be carefully rationed. I had no idea that in thirty or so years' time, miniature water filters would become available for different types of outdoor pursuits, and being able to purify water from rivers and streams would become a huge convenience.

Eventually, the upper path I was travelling on met up with the lower path again. Had I chosen that path instead on the earlier part of the walk, the experience of so many elements of nature coming together would probably have been missed. That most glorious setting further back on the path will live on in my mind for the rest of my life.

A triangulation point soon appeared on my right. This feature was shown on the map, and I fixed my exact position. The path ahead clearly headed abruptly down the cliff into a steep-sided river gulley gouging its way down to the edge of the sea. I pressed on with the eagerness of an explorer. Slithering down the cliff path, I disturbed a raven that appeared to be breakfasting on something it had pounced on in the heather. It flew off, with its bad tempered 'kraa' echoing from the deepening dell in front of me.

Birdsong floated in upon me from all directions. The highly pitched twitterings of the smaller birds, aerial melodies from the larks, even the streamlined 'scree' of swifts hunting way up in the cloudless sky for insects to feed their young, all of these sounds came together in a chaotic madrigal that made me smile and feel good about life, especially when the seagulls joined in with their raucous choruses.

I had now reached the narrow river at the bottom of the main incline. Have you noticed how some rivers wallow in their own characteristics and become memorable? This little river had plenty of that. Chinking and clinking over its rocks and pebbles, and murmuring quietly in its side pools, the river beckoned the traveller to rest awhile and enjoy this peaceful corner of the world.

With boots and socks off, I let the icy water send shock waves through my feet and up through my legs. Even my head seemed to tingle with this refreshing shock to my system. As I dangled my feet in the current, I studied the giant slabs of stone that formed an ancient bridge over the river. I wondered how many years the bridge had been there and about the people who had built it. The effort to transport such heavy granite slabs, to shape them, and to engineer them into position must have been colossal.

Two walkers appeared at this moment on the other side of the river. They waved a greeting as they crossed the small bridge. These were the first people I had seen since leaving St Ives. We chatted about the wonderful weather and the way it lent a spectacular aura to the countryside and seascape. I commented about the heat and my concern over the diminishing water reserve in my bottle. They said that I could get a refill in the hamlet of Zennor, just a few miles further on. It would mean walking inland for a mile, but there was a good pub to be enjoyed at the end of it. The morning's increasing heat persuaded me that a pint of ale could put an extra spring in my step. I thanked them, and they wished me a good journey to Penzance as they started to climb up the steep slope that I had earlier come down.

With my boots and socks back on again, my feet felt beautifully refreshed. There were no signs of blistering at this stage, and I promised myself that my feet would get a good soaking as every convenient opportunity presented itself. The next section of the walk showed up on the map as more testing than the walk up to this point. I couldn't see the path ahead from this low level on the river. Perhaps that was just as well considering that the walk so far had not been particularly easy. And now that the sun's heat radiated up from the granite rocks all around me, and lavished its overgenerous gifts from the sky above, I wondered just what lay in store for me in the miles ahead.

SIX

My tingling feet and legs felt good after their cold water therapy. Hoisting the backpack onto my shoulders didn't feel so good. The weight pulled down onto my shoulders with what seemed like extra force after my rest by the river. I looked up at the steep slope in front of me and reminded myself that this was all part of the trekking experience.

Within minutes, I had become used to the weight again, so it seemed that my body could cope with what was being thrown at it, even in the increasing heat. This thought came back towards the end of the first day's trek to taunt me.

As I rounded the bend at the top of the visible path, a striking seascape opened up. My map told me that I had reached the rocky islet and reefs of the Carracks. But what the map did not prepare me for was the seal colony around and on the islet. The black, bobbing heads of the seals moved rhythmically with the ocean's swell, and the seals snoozing on the sun-drenched rocks had probably eaten their fill of the mackerel riffling the surface of the sea all around the rocky lagoon. This was another idyllic scene to live on in my memory. What a morning to be here in Cornwall, this land of legend!

There were some steep climbs ahead. I took a parting look at the seals, wished them well, and set off up the looming cliffs. The heat had increased, and so had my water consumption, but at least Zennor offered the chance to get a refill. Looking around from the top of the climb, I could clearly see Zennor headland in the distance. This was a long, grassy-topped spit of land with rock-jagged sides, apparently much loved by the raucous seagulls.

In-between me and the headland, there cascaded a steep and rough descent followed by a long ascent up to the take-off point where the headland shot out abruptly from the main line of the coast. *Just this one last push of the morning*, I thought, *and then the mile inland to the pub.*

What wasn't apparent about the descent into this giant, bowl-like terrain surprised me. The path frequently gave way to a tumble of massive granite boulders with dangerous gaps between many of them. A false move here could lead to a bad fall or even broken limbs. I soon got the message that my trusty walking staff was of no use here, and it had to be tied carefully onto my pack, leaving me with both hands free.

These boulders were so numerous and obstructive that the descent left me drenched with sweat. I slipped forward a few times on the smoothest granite, even while taking great care. Luckily, the Vibram soles on my boots saved the day by gripping the rock firmly and stopping me from sliding any further into danger. If anyone walking by themselves had a bad accident on these rocks with no one around to help them, it would be critical. In cold weather, or with approaching nightfall, anyone falling and going into shock might not make it through the night. Absolute caution is called for on such terrain. Leaving clear information about your route and timetable with someone reliable is also of paramount importance.

The bottom of the descent came at last, but the boulders continued on the flat section of the path for a while. At least this was safer than the forward momentum of heading down the steep and prolonged slope that I had just negotiated.

Heading up the long stretch of open ground to Zennor headland came as a welcome relief. Gorse scented the air in its intoxicating way, and that lovely plant, sea thrift, decorated small areas upon and close to the rocky upthrusts. The gulls swooped and circled all around against the great blue bowl of the cloudless sky. I find it difficult to decide with seagulls whether their cry is powerfully assertive or plaintive. It often makes me think of Mr Mitchell spending hours on the sea cliffs near his home, studying the flight of seabirds and lapwings. This study was put to serious use when he designed the spitfire aircraft. His story is told in the film *The First of the Few*. What a great story that is!

The top of this climb eventually appeared. A short search revealed the signpost to Zennor, and I set off on the one-mile trek inland. Cornish miles have a reputation for being optimistic when they appear on signs and milestones, and this one happened to be a case in point. I know it was towards the end of a long morning's hot walk, but the country lane to the pub seemed almost double the distance shown.

The pub, a few cottages, and a church came into view. This really is a hamlet, yet it is also famous in its unobtrusive way. There is a carving of a mermaid on the end of one of the pews in the church, and its history is enough to bring a steady stream of tourists from all over this country and further afield to see it. Here is one version of the story:

Many years ago, the vicar of the small church had a grown-up son whose passion was to spend hours lingering out on the coast and down in the cove by the headland. He looked at the sea and just let his thoughts drift off into zen-like spaces. One day, he heard beautiful singing coming from the sea, but no one seemed to be nearby. Suddenly, a woman as beautiful as her voice emerged from the playful waves just seaward of him. It was love at first sight. She left the sea and went with him back to Zennor. I don't know what difficulties they had to overcome, but they married and stayed in the hamlet until the call of the sea lured the mermaid back to her real world. The vicar's son was distraught. He spent most of his time down at the cove thinking of her, until one day he heard her singing to him again. She beckoned to him, and he went out into the sea to follow her, never to be seen again.

The Tinner's Arm's cool stone structure loomed up in front of me with its oasis of shaded courtyard. I spotted an external tap that dripped away in a corner of the court and made a mental note of it. The pub was fairly busy, but I managed to get served in a few moments. Sitting outside in the cool shade with a pint of Cornish ale revived me and prepared me for the considerable distance that still lay ahead on this first day's walk. I had a pleasant conversation with one or two other customers, refilled my water bottle, and saddled up ready to take on the next part of this coastal adventure.

SEVEN

The early afternoon walk back to the coast became even hotter than the morning's walk. Luckily, I had a brimmed bush hat that kept the sun out of my eyes and off my head and neck. This sunshine needed care in case of heatstroke.

Back near the coast again, I found the signpost for the coastal path and followed its direction down numerous steps to a gushing river at the bottom, a pleasant spot indeed. Its little waterfall cascaded over a high rock, and just listening to it made me feel cooler. I gathered up handfuls of water from the river and splashed it joyfully into my face and over my upper body. Now I was 'good to go'.

The rough terrain rose steeply from the river. I was no more than a minute into the ascent when a young adder shot out from grassy cover on my left, slithered over the toecap of my leading boot, and dived for cover on my right. My rapid heart rate thudded throughout every part of me. *Don't go into shock*, I heard myself ordering my whole body. The sight of a fully grown adder coiled on the path a few yards further ahead didn't make the situation any more tranquil. This second snake seemed to be sleeping, drugged by the sun.

I had seen adders before when walking on Dartmoor but never in such close proximity. The knowledge I had of this reptile suggested that when they come out of their winter sleep, they are often bad tempered, but their level of poison is relatively low. Even so, that level of poison can still cause you a lot of pain and distress. The other aspect is that a sudden bite from this snake can induce a heart attack brought on by the shock. Later in the year, after several months of coiled sunbathing, the adder's poison increases markedly.

Looking at the snake still coiled just up the path from me, I needed a strategy to get past it. The ground on both sides of the pathway could easily have harboured more of these creatures, so I needed to persuade this one to move away. Whether it is true, I don't know, but something in my mind reminded me that adders are probably deaf. This is why extra care is necessary when walking in areas like this. Coastal footpaths are among the adder's favourite domains, and they love to soak up the sunshine on open ground typical of the footpath right in front of me.

It seems that if the adder knows danger is approaching it will quickly get out of the way. But being deaf, detecting approaching danger could be a challenge. Vibration is the answer. When you are walking into longer grass and vegetation that is bending over your pathway, stamp your boots down into the ground to cause such a disturbance that it will alert the dozing snake. This should do the trick, but should I try my luck with it?

I marched cautiously on, stamping my feet and banging the end of my walking staff forcefully into the ground. The creature suddenly zipped into life, glared venomously at me, and took off into the ground cover. I could see its progress for a few feet, then it was gone into the deeper vegetation. That experience was unforgettable. It was several years later that a regular walker in this area told me that Zennor is a notorious area for adders, but they are far more afraid of us than we are of them, and that is saying something.

* * *

By this time, the sweat oozed out of me. The sunshine poured down relentlessly, and the big, padded hip belt of the pack started to rub the area under my ribcage. I decided to unfasten the belt and let my shoulders take the strain of the harness to give my midriff a rest.

After the climb up from Zennor, the relatively flat terrain came as a relief. The first close-up signs of this area's mining heritage started to appear. Some of these are close to the path, and the signs warn of the dangers. Uncapped mineshafts are a particular hazard, and reports of dogs falling into these are unfortunately quite regular. If the dogs are lucky, they will live through a fall and be rescued by the special teams of people who know what they are doing. Occasionally, walkers also inadvertently fall into these shafts. Clearly, it is vital to keep to the footpath, and I vowed to do just that.

It wasn't long before the headland of Gurnard's Head came into view. This is a striking section of coast with an interesting history. The tricky rock faces present climbers with a real challenge. So much so that the area came to be used regularly by Royal Marine commandos for cliff assault training and general climbing skills. From a distance, the challenges on those rock faces look very testing indeed.

Looking beyond Gurnard's Head, I saw Pendeen Watch lighthouse in the far distance. The afternoon had already accelerated into my speculative schedule, and without a tent on this trip, I needed to be in St Just by early evening to find accommodation for the night. Failing that, I would probably be sleeping in a hedge on the outskirts of the town. My map showed that the distance still remaining to be covered before arriving at the town was considerable.

I increased my pace a little under the searing heat of the sun, and the reflected glare off the placid sea added to my burden. It was about this time that my shoulders started to object threateningly to the weight of my unsupported backpack. In the effort to temporarily relieve the chafing of my waist by the pack's hip belt,

I had pushed my shoulders too far. Perhaps if I fastened the belt again, my shoulders would quickly forgive me.

The plod towards Pendeen Watch found me starting to call on my reserves of endurance. With the time now constantly in mind, I pressed on as well as I could. Stopping for a quick breather at Pendeen gave me the opportunity to admire the great view along the coast and the awesome reef offshore. It was this reef area that the lighthouse warned mariners to avoid at all costs. But one thing about the sea fairly close-in to the rocky shoreline held my particular attention. A band of discoloured water lazed along the coast with the tidal current. The band was a few yards wide and reddish-brown in colour. I had never seen anything like this before, and I had spent most of my life living near the sea and tidal rivers; I found the answer to this enigma about thirty minutes later.

From Pendeen Watch the terrain became quite level. In fact, it was some of the most pleasant and easy walking ground of the day so far. It became easier to push my pace along in an effort to keep to the schedule.

Looming up in the near distance, an arid landscape appeared with industrial buildings that looked abandoned. These were the old mine workings of Geevor. It seemed that mining had been carried on here since the Middle Ages. I could imagine how bleak and cold this place might be in the winter, but today it was like the sun's anvil. As fascinating as this area was, I reminded myself that I must press on if I was to get accommodation for the night. Then a local walker drew level with me. I took the opportunity to ask about the wide band of coloured sea water coursing with the current from just off the Geevor coast to Pendeen Watch and probably beyond. This was seepage from old mine workings going over a mile out under the sea from Geevor. What an amazing feat of mine engineering! As an afterthought, I asked the elderly gentleman if he could recommend overnight accommodation in St Just. He knew just the guest house for a weary traveller.

At the top of the climb up from Geevor, the ground started to be more friendly again. I could see that the coast had started to curve around towards Cape Cornwall and eventually, Land's End. This encouraged me to shrug off the aches in my shoulders caused by my earlier release of the hip belt. In fact, the aching was by now quite bad, and I wondered if this would become a problem tomorrow on the long trek to Penzance. A good night's sleep was certainly called for.

Cape Cornwall came nicely into view. St Just is not far inland from the Cape, and it was just approaching 5pm; I would be in the town by 6.30pm with a reasonable chance of finding a guest house with a vacancy. The sun's power had started to lessen just as my energy level dipped sharply in sympathy. The weight of the backpack bore down on me remorselessly. What's this? Surely, I wasn't feeling sorry for myself? No, but I did resolve to be far more Spartan with the gear I packed in future.

St Just came into view – beautiful! I found the excellent guest house that had been recommended to me and booked in for the night. The husband-and-wife team running the house suggested one or two good restaurants within easy walking distance, and this sounded ideal. A good meal, a large glass of wine, then back to the guest house for a well-earned sleep had great appeal, but first I needed a long shower after such an exhilarating but exhausting day.

The warm water from the shower made me light-headed with pure relaxation. I intended to get dressed for the evening straight away, but the desire to just totally relax on the bed was overwhelming; I granted myself just five minutes before changing and heading out for an evening meal. My pocket watch showed the time as ten minutes to seven.

* * *

I suddenly jolted into consciousness. It was now seven o'clock, according to the watch that was still in the palm of my hand. No time to waste if I wanted to get a meal that evening. Then I noticed how the light in the room had changed its quality to become fresher and brighter. Surely it couldn't be? But it was. Morning had broken, like the first morning, as the old hymn tells us. I had slept for twelve hours through sheer exhaustion; nothing like that had ever happened to me before, but I definitely felt the benefit of it.

Breakfast was very welcome as I hadn't eaten anything since lunch the previous day. The hosts were so obliging that they even served me a second full English breakfast as they thought I was starving. So, with my energy replenished, and with the two-litre water bottle refilled, I made my way out onto the street to start the second, and final, day of the trek on this my first ever solo trekking adventure.

EIGHT

The problems became apparent immediately. First of all, my feet were sore. My legs ached down their full length. But the worst thing was the pain in my shoulders paying me back for not buckling up the hip belt on the last part of yesterday's walk. As I walked past the bus stop for Penzance, human frailty almost won the day, especially with the bus just about to leave. My love of the outdoors won the contest, and I resolved that I would complete this walk to Penzance, no matter what. I popped into the local shop and stocked up on some snacks and a Cornish pasty for lunch. Nothing could stop me now!

A short walk through St Just got me onto the coastal footpath again, and the weather beamed its springtime freshness down on me. After a little while, I saw Land's End shimmering in the distance. I had never been to Land's End before, and my anticipation of being there on such a day as this made me forget for a while my aches and pains. But first, I needed to walk a fair distance along Whitesand Bay to the fascinating village of Sennen Cove.

I was enjoying the walk along the path when suddenly there welled up a rage of raucous squawking from the massive platforms of rock on the edge of the sea far below me. To my utter amazement, the commotion that shredded the peace of the morning came from a mass of seagulls attacking a male fox running for its life over the rocks. He had presumably been caught robbing eggs or maybe taking a seagull chick from the gulls' colony. The gulls were furious. They dived on the fox repeatedly, slicing at him with their large, weapon-like beaks. This was no mere warning. It looked to me as if the seagulls intended to hunt the fox until it dropped. The hunt moved away from my position so quickly that I didn't see what eventually happened. The whole scene reminded me of Alfred Hitchcock's *The Birds*. Gulls may look fairly harmless, but I saw a different side of their natures that morning.

The coastal footpath continued in its usual way for a couple of much quieter miles, then surprised me by dropping right down onto the sandy beach. Playful waves slithered up the sand towards me, hissed their final gasp to the glistening tideline before slipping quietly back into the tropical blue-green of the sea. Seagulls floated up and over the lazy incoming waves, then slid down smoothly into the troughs. *Were any of these a part of the earlier hunting party?* I wondered.

I looked back at the Brisons, a huge reef lying off Cape Cornwall. There was a lot of aerial activity high up over the reef's two massive rocks, and what I saw next was amazing. Huge numbers of gannets were diving from a great height onto several shoals of fish all around the reef. The gannets javelined down from a few hundred feet in a fast vertical dive to snatch their prey at a depth of up to several feet, probably mackerel or the large sand eel called launce. What a sight! Nature had clearly designed these birds to be perfect for what I had just witnessed.

Walking on the big, sandy beach presented quite a change from the coastal footpath. Instead of a clearly defined path, one could roam around a lot more, down by the sea's margin some of the time and further up the beach when the mood took me. Eventually, Sennen village loomed up right in front of me. It is a neat village with many a tale to tell of shipwrecks, fishing, and in more recent times, the holiday trade. Still unspoiled in its simple beauty, its cottages and fishing gear stores moulded the morning's sunlight and shadows into an artist's dream. I fell in love with this place. Being a keen sea angler, I pondered on what it would be like to spend a day on a placid sea, drift fishing around the many reefs just offshore.

I stopped for a rest and a cup of tea at a lovely teashop looking right out over the bay stretching from Sennen to Cape Cornwall back in the far distance. Reflecting on the things I had seen that glorious morning assured me more than ever that backpacking was one of the things I had been born to do. What a pity that earning a living had to get in the way of that!

The path up to Land's End presented the steepest climb of the morning so far. Apart from the occasional walker, I had this part of the walk to myself. When I arrived at the headland itself, there was a shocking sight. There were dozens of swallows on the turf all around the path, and there were others flying in from over the sea and falling out of the sky exhausted. One swallow couldn't even find the strength to avoid crashing into me. I held it to my chest and felt its little heart pounding against me. It looked up into my eyes, and I was choked with emotion for the exhausted little mite.

These birds had probably flown in stages from Africa, and they had just completed their last big part of the journey by flying over to Cornwall from France, or perhaps Spain or Portugal. While I was pondering on this Homeric journey, the swallows on the ground and on the rocks near me started to revive. Within a few more minutes, some had started to fly again. They seemed eager to explore their new surroundings. My new friend, who was still clinging to me, watched his companions set off again and became restless. I wished it every good fortune, stroked it one more time, and lifted it away from my chest so that it could fly away and join the others. Off it flew with a laboured spread of its wings, but it had clearly recovered a lot of its strength in that short time. The experience of helping that little palpitating parcel of epic life was another memory to treasure.

I walked on, thinking about all the things that had happened to me so far on this walk, and realised that I was not the same person who had set off from St Ives a little over twenty-four hours ago. Perhaps Hamlet was right when he said:

'There are more things in heaven and earth, Horatio, than are dreamt of in your philosophy'.

Thoughts of the rest of this day's journey started floating into my mind when a voice broke into my consciousness. "You are miles away, Eric. What are you thinking about?" It was Arthur talking to me back in St Ives.

While our group had stopped to adjust rucksacks, have a quick drink of water, and take a parting look at Porthmeor Beach, I had gone back over thirty years to relive the very first time I had walked this same route. I had time-travelled over that precious day and a half in just a few treasured moments. "Well, Arthur, I was just thinking how fortunate we all are to be here at the start of this great walk. Let's hope that the weather will be kind to us."

Arthur chuckled, looked sceptical, and off we all went.

* * *

We moved away from Porthmeor Beach at a good, steady pace towards the take-off point for the coast path. This was soon reached, and we set out towards the small headlands ahead of us. The first climb of the day came into view, and I could see already that we had split into three distinct groups with different preferred walking speeds. Group walking often shows this tendency, but it doesn't usually lead to any real problem. Being a walker who almost always prefers to walk alone, this was an unusual experience for me, so I must learn to adapt, especially with the expedition to Kilimanjaro set up for just five months' time. Added to that, I would be starting the training walks with Jon in one month.

Arthur was having some eye trouble caused by cataracts in both eyes. His operation for the first eye was imminent, but he considered that this walk shouldn't present him with any insurmountable problems. Under normal circumstances, I think that would be a reasonable decision. But what we didn't bargain for was the deep and squelchy quagmire waiting for us just around the next bend in the path.

The dreadfully wet winter that we had just come through led us to expect some muddy conditions on the path. Towards the top of this first climb, we saw the first mud of the day, and what an eye-opener that was! Thick, glutinous, and a lot of it, does not do justice to the mud that confronted us. In over thirty years of walking these paths, I had never seen this coast path in such a challenging state. The real problem seemed to be that the path at this point was a fair distance below the top of the hillside that sloped down to the coast. You can imagine that all the reservoired winter rainwater would take a long time to seep gradually out of the soil above the path. And the path, being cut into the hillside, acted as a release point for a lot of that water. Water and loose soil get together to form mud, and as people walk the pathway, the mud gets more and more churned up into a quagmire.

We slithered and grunted our way through what mud was visible, but the sight that confronted us when we rounded the bend in the pathway showed us that the muddy section had only just got under way. What lay ahead was ghastly and grim to say the least. Surely the miles of path that stretched before us couldn't be this bad, could they?

We came to what looked like a fairly gentle slope leading up to a closed gate across the path, but what appeared to be a solid-looking surface from a distance proved to be anything but that. The marsh in front of us was running with water, and the mud deepened the more we tried to reach the gate. I suddenly recalled that my gaiters were in the pack, and I put them on, while cursing myself for not putting them on sooner. This set the trend, and those in our group who had gaiters with them did the same. This great bank of mud became even deeper as we slid and splodged up to the gate, and I speculated that this was the result of a herd of cattle milling about near the gate waiting to be fed. In fact, we could see cattle in the field the other side of the gate as well.

One by one, we reached the gate and found that the ground the other side tended to be muddy but not quite as bad as what we had just traversed. Shortly after this, there came a section of the path that skittered down a muddy slope. This clearly needed even greater care as we were all slipping and sliding. This is where fate paid us a visit. Arthur, who was doing very well up to this point, got his foot caught up in a bramble that had grown out into just the wrong position and fell forward into the mud but twisted on his way down and ended up more or less on his back. His anorak bore the brunt of it and became smothered in some of Cornwall's finest saturated soil. Dave and Karen managed to get Arthur upright again, but his rucksack had also borne the brunt of the mud slide. Luckily, Arthur is made of tough and resolute stuff and quickly got back into his stride, as can be seen from this picture of Arthur blazing the trail over the granite boulders that are so much a feature of the coastal footpath:

*Arthur, Brian, and Dave negotiating the first
of the many boulder fields on this journey*

The walk so far had marked differences from the very first time I walked this route, and just to emphasise that, the clouds began to gather, and the temperature started to drop.

We reached the river at the bottom of the steep slope and stopped for a photo shoot on the stone bridge:

Our group on the Cornish granite clapper bridge: Brian Rowe; Karen Mckee; Dave Mckee; Pearl Gilby; Richard Jackelman; and Arthur Hatch

Unlike the serene setting of my first visit to this spot, the river today was a jostling torrent rushing furiously down steeply to the nearby sea. I didn't feel inclined to bathe my feet this time, but this sheltered spot offered a convenient place for a short break.

On we pressed towards the Carracks seal colony. The seals were still there, but only one or two bobbed their heads up above the surface of the sea. By this time, the breeze had sharpened its edge coming in from the sea, and we were glad of our jumpers and anoraks, even though they could be rather too warm on the longer and steeper climbs.

Having climbed up from the path overlooking the Carracks, I knew what we were in for next. The giant granite boulders with the dangerous gaps between were waiting for us. We all joined in to help one another over this tricky descent over the boulders. Right on cue, the drizzle started at that moment to dampen the rocks we were scrambling over to make them slippery, but we eventually completed the descent.

We reached the bottom of the boulder field to everyone's relief. There were still more boulders to negotiate, but at least they lay on a much flatter plane. I was sweating by this time, probably because of the concentration needed to get over these leg- and ankle-trapping monsters.

Our next destination was Zennor. I knew that Richard and Pearl liked pressing forward, so I didn't make a big thing about the pleasures of the Tinner's Arms for a lunchtime glass of ale. Added to that, we still had a long way to go before our overnight accommodation. This had been booked by Karen at the Land's End Youth Hostel. Why it is called by that name I am not sure. The hostel is much closer to St Just than Land's End, but it is still a long walk whichever way you cut it, and we really did need to press on after a quick lunch break by the river near Zennor. But before we headed down the long, steep slope to the river, I pointed out that the signpost showed us that after a morning of slithering, sliding, and hard walking, we had only covered six miles. That was difficult to believe after all the effort we had put in. The distance shown must be another notorious example of 'Cornish miles' again!

The lunch break took our minds off the morning of mud and chilly winds, so much so that Dave and Karen showed us their romantic side by posing for a kiss in front of the little waterfall teeming down the hillside from Zennor.

We pressed on up the long climb from the river to the high ground. This is where I had encountered the two adders on that first epic walk, but today the chilly wind and lack of sun must have persuaded them to stay coiled up in their sanctuaries to dream of better weather.

My map showed that we had about another seven miles to walk before our next prominent point; this was Pendeen Watch. I assumed that when we reached the higher ground the terrain would be a lot less muddy. Alas! That was a forlorn hope. The narrow pathways were often walled in on one side and with a thick hedge on the other side. This left us with no choice – we had to negotiate the churned-up mud as well as we could. Oh! What fun.

We plodded on with the sky becoming increasingly grey and the sea breeze hinting that rain was imminent. There hadn't been any rain so far, apart from just a gentle drizzle that only lasted a few minutes. We were thankful for small mercies.

Since leaving Zennor, Pearl and Richard had hit their preferred pace and had gradually gone ahead. They were now out of sight. It was beginning to look like a big ask for our remaining five to reach the hostel at St Just by 7pm for the evening meal, unless we increased the pace considerably. We knew that Brian's level of fitness was high, so he was the ideal choice to strike out for the hostel. There was a good chance that he could get to the hostel in good time to ask for our evening meal to be delayed due to the way our enemy, the mud, had slowed us down most of the way from St Ives. There was also a good chance that Richard and Pearl would get to the hostel in time to arrange for a later meal, but they had never walked this route before, and route-finding beyond Geevor mining area can be rather tricky on the first attempt. Brian readily agreed to take on this task, and I volunteered to go with him. If I could keep up with his pace, it would be great extra training for my expedition in five months' time.

Brian is a very fit cyclist who has been on a number of solo long-distance trips in this country and in Europe. He is about nine months younger than I am, and just like me, he realises that being in our seventies and still fit and healthy, we should, if anything, take fitness even more seriously than we did in our earlier years. We set off at a mercurial pace and talked about all sorts of topics. I have never been into cycling, but I was interested in hearing about Brian's varied experiences on his biking adventures.

The terrain we covered on the way to Pendeen Watch certainly tested us, especially when we hit more muddy and steep areas. But we eventually arrived at the impressive lighthouse, with a view of the equally impressive offshore reefs. At this stage, a short rest would have been good, but we remembered that time was against us. I knew from previous walks over this same route that it was possible to reach the hostel from St Ives by 6pm, but the mud had slowed us down a lot on this occasion. We crossed our fingers that the second day would be kinder to us.

Our route from the Pendeen lighthouse was by way of a narrow road that pointed inland. We started out along this road, but after a short while I realised that something was not right; we were too far away from the coast. Retracing our steps for a minute or so, I could see what had happened. The very small signpost that showed the continuation of the footpath had been repositioned away from the road and was partly obscured by ferns.

Now that we were on the right route again, we pushed up the pace a little. The terrain now became a lot more open and undulating instead of the steep slopes of the walk up to this point. There had still not been any rain, and the sky showed signs of granting us a sunny evening.

Coming into view, we saw the Geevor Tin Mine. Its stark, industrial landscape in the setting of a great seascape never ceases to astonish me. The sun came through just in time to highlight the aridity of Geevor's massive hillside with its mine workings, some dating back to the Middle Ages. There was no trace today of the red-brown slick floating up from the undersea mine workings and streaming out with the tide. Brian had never seen that, so I described what I had seen on my first walk along this section of coast and had seen several times on other walks here since that time.

On we walked, and the going became relatively easier. I had always noticed that when carrying my fully laden backpack for camping, it was just about at this point that tiredness really set in after carrying that extra weight all day. We were only carrying our daypacks today, but the feeling of having been on a long walk since early morning still started to have an effect.

The coast path wound on for a while before curving around more to a southerly direction. This gave us a splendid view of Cape Cornwall. It was still quite a way off, yet we knew that the hostel was not too far away from the cape. I checked the time. We were not going to get to the hostel by the mealtime but perhaps twenty to thirty minutes after the meal had started. At least we were booked in for the meal. It was unfortunate that we only had a central booking telephone number with us and not the actual number for the hostel. Karen had booked the accommodation and meals and had the number with her. Unfortunately, getting a phone signal on the coast path can be hit and miss. Perhaps she will be lucky enough to pick up a signal and get through to the hostel to explain our difficulty.

Cape Cornwall is a striking jewel in the seascape leading up to Land's End in the far distance. Our plan was to reach Land's End by late morning the following day, and this would give us a good chance of being in Penzance before dark. We took a moment to admire the low sun on its journey into the west. It seemed likely that we would get to the hostel with plenty of daylight to spare.

Our route took us down into Priest's Cove by Cape Cornwall. The salty tang in the gentle air rippled up from the crab pots and fishing nets, the working gear, and the huge fronds of kelp exposed on the rocks by the outgoing tide. There weren't any gannets working around the offshore Brisons reef this time, but my thoughts went back to when I first saw them spearing into the sea from great heights after mackerel and the greater sand eel.

Boat fishing from this cove is not an easy task. There is a small, powered winch to assist in the hauling of boats up the rutted slipway, but the boatmen find it far easier to help one another with the launching and recovery of their craft. When I look out at the glittering sea and the rocky nature of the seabed, the lure of fishing this area makes me feel excited. Marginal weather would be quite another matter for the fishermen on such a potentially dangerous stretch of coast, yet this has to be reckoned against the need to earn a living. Needless to say, fishing is in their blood.

Brian and I set off again on yet another steep and prolonged climb. I was feeling the strain by this time, but Brian's fitness allowed him to keep striding out. I made a mental note to concentrate on even more leg-strengthening work when I got back to the gym. The thought of Kilimanjaro sprang into my mind. The trekking demands would have to be met and overcome, or I would be joining the trekkers sent back to base to await the return of the rest of the group. How disappointing this would be after months of training! This thought gave me a sudden burst of energy, and I went forward with new vigour.

The steep climb gave way to a long section of flat terrain with gorgeous evening views of the sea and countryside. There were even some ancient burial chambers and cairns. To add to this glorious evening, we heard a cuckoo in the distance.

We eventually arrived at a point on the path that gave us a view of what appeared to be the hostel. It was perched higher up on the hillside overlooking the valley we were in that led down to the sea. There weren't any signposts for the hostel, and the way to get to the place wasn't at all clear. I wondered about all the other tired walkers who had come in on this same path over the years and didn't have any local knowledge to help them get to the hostel.

We explored any likely paths, but they quickly led us away from our destination. As a last resort, we headed up the steep tarmac road. The road took a bend to the left as the hill flattened out, but a signpost told us that we were heading towards St Just. It was clear that we were also heading away from the general direction of what we thought was the hostel. We just didn't need this at the end of the day, especially as we were thirty minutes past the official mealtime and in need of a shower.

Retracing our steps to the top of the hill, I noticed a narrow and quite overgrown lane, slinking between trees and shrubs. In the absence of any other ideas, we tried it. Within a few paces, we found a windblown sign telling us that the hostel was straight ahead. Made it!

* * *

Just as we entered the reception area, we met up with Pearl and Richard; they had arrived here about an hour and a half ago. The small, unobtrusive sign that we had nearly missed at Pendeen Watch had quite understandably not been spotted by Richard and Pearl. By the time they had covered the two miles inland to Pendeen village, it was quite obvious to them that they had overshot the take-off point for the coastal path. Just as they were replenishing their supplies at the local mini-market, the St Just bus arrived outside the shop. This was too tempting to resist, and they jumped on board. Having asked for directions in St Just, they made their way easily to the hostel.

It was good to meet up with our two friends again, but we wondered if they had any news about the other three. There had been an attempted call from Karen's mobile phone to the hostel reception, but it dropped out after a few seconds. Just at that moment, the outer door opened and in came our 'lost' compatriots. Faces relaxed into smiles of relief, and the tensions melted away. They had found the take-off point for the coastal footpath at Pendeen Watch without too much trouble. I had repositioned the sign to help them find the route. Then, having reached Geevor Tin Mine, they knew that the odds were stacked against them for getting to the hostel in reasonable time for the evening meal. The good news was that they had found the walking had improved greatly since the worst of the mud had receded on this different section of coast.

The map showed that they could cut across country to St Just. Once in the town, they could make their way to the hostel and save quite a lot of time, so that is what they did. Their route led them out to the main road into St Just, but they hadn't bargained for the long and steep hill that would take them up into the town. Nevertheless, it was a good plan, and here we all were in time for a very quick shower before the supper that the staff had kindly rearranged for us in the circumstances.

Our five guys shared a dormitory with bunk beds, and the two girls had a private room with two bunks. I felt that no matter if there were to be snoring or not during the night, there was just no way that I would not sleep after all that fresh air and sustained exercise of the day.

We all met up in the small dining room where the aroma from the kitchen reminded us just how hungry we were. As there was going to be a short delay, we did the sensible thing and bought our drinks. The bench seats were hard, but the sheer relief of sitting down at the table was wonderful.

The chef served up our meals to us in person. What he must have thought when he saw the scene in front of him, I cannot imagine. No sooner had the plates touched down on the table than the seven of us swooped on the lasagne like St Ives seagulls swooping on an unguarded bag of fish and chips. It became a case of the survival of the fittest, and we were all pretty fit!

The food went down well. The drinks went down as swiftly as a forlorn river meeting a vast area of hot, dry, sandy desert. One thing was certain: we hadn't realised up to that point just how seriously dehydrated we all were. As the drinks flowed, so did the stories, jokes, and ribbing. Companionship had not been lacking during the day's walk, but it now reached a higher level. Meeting and talking with these friends in the gym itself was one thing, but a new bond had been built up between us in our common enterprise. All good things come to an end, and it was time to have a last drink before getting a well-deserved night's sleep to replenish the energy for the next day's even longer walk from St Just hostel to Penzance.

Then, the unexpected happened. The pleasant Dutch family sitting at the next table were wide-eyed with amazement. Their mouths gaped open, and it was hard to tell if their expressions were that of horror or complete disbelief. All of this was caused by Richard. As a final rounding off for the evening, he had decided to give us a rendering of two of his favourite sea shanties. He sings with a popular sea shanty group in Devon, and his singing really is good. I guess that our dining companions from the Netherlands were totally unaware of this maritime art form. In any event, Richard received a great ovation from all the diners, including our Dutch friends. Now it really was time to hit the sack.

We five guys started to prepare for bed when I stunned the other four by donning my silk dressing gown in order to cross the corridor to pay a visit to the toilet. It seemed to me like a good idea, when in a mixed hostel with shared facilities, to pack a very lightweight dressing gown. Dave, who can always be relied on to see the funny side of things, shouted out that I looked just like Mr Bridger. Never having seen the film *The Italian Job* with Michael Caine, I didn't realise that Noel Coward, aka Mr Bridger, was Mr Big and almost always wore a similar dressing gown to mine when he was in prison serving his sentence and running the show from his quite luxurious cell. Can you believe it? This little episode did the rounds back at the gym, much to the members' amusement. Thank you, Dave, I hope to return the favour some day!

Sleep overtook us all. There were certain pointed comments the next morning about a phantom snorer in the room. Being an occasional snorer myself, I naturally thought the remarks were aimed at me. My relief came quickly when the culprit was named and shamed; no names, no pack drill as the old army saying goes.

Breakfast was a bit of a scramble, and that doesn't just mean the eggs. The queue for coffee caused the main hold up as that queue intersected the main breakfast queue and led to some confusion. All was resolved, and we sat down together again to enjoy this welcome meal in preparation for the hard walking that lay ahead of us. We gathered up our gear from the rooms, collected our pre-ordered packed lunches, and met up outside in delightful sunshine. Richard wanted a group photo in front of the wall of the hostel, with the imposing sign of the Youth Hostel Association in a prominent position. Now we were all set and ready to go. The next stop would be Sennen Cove.

NINE

We picked up the best route to rejoin the coastal footpath without any problems, and the ground conditions were good. The sun continued to shine down in a friendly way on the impressive seascape and on the sea itself with its lazy swell waves. This was more like it after the wet and mournful months of winter.

Sennen seemed a long way away when we first saw it. Positioned in a cove at the point where Whitesand Bay curls around to nudge up against the great bulwark of Land's End, it had instant appeal in weather such as we were experiencing. This gave us a spur to increase our speed. We knew that today would be a challenge to get to Penzance before the evening light receded. Walking on the often-tricky terrain of the coastal footpath after dark didn't strike us as being a great idea. On we pressed with the knowledge that there would probably be enough time to grab a quick cup of tea in Sennen before climbing up the steep slope to get to Land's End towards the end of the morning.

As the pathway led us down from the cliffs to the beach, we realised how much traction was lost by walking on sand instead of the hard-packed nature of the path; the pace slowed down noticeably. However, it wasn't long before our attention got caught up with something else. We found ourselves walking a gauntlet between the sandcastle builders and the numerous surfers making their way down to the small swell waves massaging the beach at its tideline. I suppose surfing is like fishing; you don't have to catch the perfect wave, or even a promising wave, to have a good day's surfing, just as you don't have to catch fish to have a good day's fishing.

We stopped for some group photos on the beach with a lovely blue sky overhead. Arthur was smiling and was much improved. His eye problems weren't much of a burden to him today because, so far, there had been virtually no mud to contend with. The whole panorama of the beach and the village, with the huge bulk of the Land's End headland in the background, made the whole walk, and especially this morning, seem so worthwhile:

Richard, Brian, Me, Arthur, Karen, and Pearl on Sennen Surf Beach

There happened to be an appealing cafe just as we reached the top of the slipway into the village, so mugs of tea and the odd chocolate bar for energy seemed the obvious thing to go for. Being such a sun-sparkling morning, we took our teas outside by the beach wall and looked out over the shimmering bay. This was an idyllic Cornish morning; one to remember for a long time.

We dragged ourselves away reluctantly and walked through the village towards the big climb that would take us eventually to Land's End. I was intrigued to see quite a collection of sea-angling kayaks in and around the car park at the end of the village. The kayakers were preparing their craft for angling trips in the bay, and I envied them enormously. I have a chart of this area, and the seabed looks fascinating. There are spectacular reefs above and below water with promising sandy gullies running between those reefs. This is classic flatfish country. It also has all the signs of being a good area for bass and definitely pollack. On a day such as this day, there shouldn't be much risk as long as one is sensible. In riskier weather conditions, these coastal waters could be frightening. You just have to grab the good opportunities when they arise.

As I mused by the slipway, the others had started to make their way up the steep cliff path. I put on an extra turn of speed and caught them up. My breathing had accelerated considerably, but my leg muscles seemed to be working well. Several walkers were making their way up the slope, and just as many were coming down, a popular day.

We reached Land's End and saw it in all its glory. I visualised Mount Kilimanjaro way out over the Atlantic in the direction of Africa and remembered that I was here today in training to climb that famous peak in five months' time. The view seawards is truly spectacular and is probably worth it for all the walkers, cyclists, runners, intrepid invalids in their wheelchairs, and vintage car enthusiasts who often make the long journey from John O' Groats on the far north coast of Scotland. I took a last lingering look at the Longships Lighthouse on the shark's teeth of a reef about a mile and a half off Land's End. It was standing out like a striking jewel in an aquamarine setting within a ring of creamy surf to dramatise its presence. But time was of the essence, and we had to press on to Penzance over the coastal miles that lay waiting for us.

After Land's End, we strode out with a spring in our steps… for a while. Then we came to the first of the long flights of steps up steep cliffs. This was the first of many that day, and some of them were exhausting, especially if one didn't get the pacing and breathing just right; just what I needed for the big climbs over the six days on Kilimanjaro in September. Part of the difficulty lay in the uneven spacing of the steps and their different heights from one step to the next. But I should make it clear that these steps really were the result of massive efforts over the years by countless volunteers. Construction must have been tough going in view of the broken ground and the twists and turns designed into the path in an effort to take a lot of the steepness out of the climbs. Climbing many of these paths in wet and muddy conditions without the aid of the steps would be much more difficult. So, thank you to all the generous people who gave their time and energy to this great project.

* * *

We eventually arrived at the little cove and hamlet of Porthgwarra, another striking old Cornish name. This looked like a good place for our lunch break, and there was even a small general shop with outside garden facilities available. There were benches and picnic tables for customers, so Richard ordered tea for us all and even got permission for us to have our packed lunches at the table while we rested. Richard's charm is legendary.

After a quick lunch, we strode out again on the pathway. Right on cue, we were faced at once with a steep and slippery climb up the ominous cliff. The next port of call would be Porthcurno. Just before reaching the village, we came to the open-air Minack Theatre. It is difficult to imagine a theatre being in a more atmospheric setting. The amphitheatre is carved into the rock, and the stage has the great expanse of sea for a backdrop. Productions here include the plays of Shakespeare, famous musicals, Greek drama, and the work of other playwrights.

I was on a weekend literature course in Somerset on one occasion when a gentleman who was also on our course told me about his almost fanatical following of the productions at the Minack Theatre. He remembered one with particular clarity. It happened to be a production of *South Pacific*. The weather didn't look too promising, but the show went ahead. When the lead female singer started singing 'I'm Gonna Wash That Man Right Outa My Hair', the angry clouds hurled down a mighty downpour. In fact, the raindrops were so vicious that they bounced two or three feet off the ground. The cast struggled on for a while longer before it had to be abandoned. In the meantime, the gentleman I was talking with had become saturated to the extent that the water just ran out of him.

He dragged himself and all the extra weight of the rainwater back up the muddy hillside to the paddling pool of a car park. Unfortunately, he didn't have any spare clothing with him. Rather than risk developing a cold, or worse, on his drive back to Falmouth, he decided to strip off all his clothes and turn up the car's heating system to maximum. But, as he drove along in the nude, the thought suddenly struck him that he had better not get involved in an accident or attract the attention of the police for fear of the sheer embarrassment and possible police action in view of the public decency law. I am pleased to report that he arrived home without any problems. He never goes to the Minack now without a fully waterproof anorak and waterproof trousers. He backs this up with a large towel and spare clothing which he leaves in the car.

From the Minack, we headed down to the sandy beach of Porthcurno with all its rich history. Its chief claim to fame is its location as the point from which the first transatlantic cable snaked out from the stern of a cable-laying ship on the long ocean journey to America. Since that first massive undertaking, several more ocean cables have furrowed up and down Porthcurno's sandy beach to be given a home in the cable terminal station nearby. That, by the way, is an astonishing quantity of copper stretching to America and other countries.

By this stage of the trek, we had toughed it out for about ten miles since leaving the hostel at St Just, although it seemed like a lot further than that. The mud had become our squelchy companion again. It didn't even let up on the flights of testing steps that we encountered. However, the sun had gradually convinced us that summer had simmered its way into this damp spring, if only as a temporary promise of what the next few months might bring. This made me think of something I read. It seems that along the west and north coasts of Scotland, a typical old saying has it that their northerly climes have nine months of winter and three months of bad weather. We must be grateful that our climate here in the far south-west is kinder than that… usually.

Our path took us eventually down into Penberth Cove, with its little river and its stepping stones. This sort of scene is usually a trigger to get the cameras out, and this is exactly what some of our group did. Being in the digital age, Dave also used his camera's video to record the scene as we all hopped across from stone to stone. Not one of us slipped and fell into the shallow river, and I could see the disappointment on Dave's face; just imagine his joy if he could have shown a video of that back at the gym!

On we plodded for another three miles across hilly terrain with more steep steps. Then we came to a totally uncharacteristic section of coastline. First of all, there were trees. These gave us some shade from the afternoon sun, which, by this time, had coaxed the atmosphere to become sauna-like. A brook chuckled its way through the woodland out to the nearby seashore, and just over the brook, an imposing cottage came into view. This was the tiny hamlet of St Loy. What a super location, we all thought! But whether or not it could be a convenient place to live was another story.

Our path took us right down onto the granite turmoil of a beach from hell. Huge boulders cluttered our route for perhaps two hundred metres before the path could be clearly seen to climb away from the beach and into the green countryside again.

We didn't need to be warned to be cautious when scrabbling over these boulders; they presented a clear and present danger. Each of us glided, jumped, and eased ourselves over this strange colony of shoulder to shoulder rocks with the gaping voids between them. A lack of concentration could easily become a leg-breakingly shocking experience. I looked around to see how the others were progressing and nearly tumbled down into one of the waiting traps myself. *Come on! Think! Concentrate!* I ordered myself.

I am glad to say that everyone reached the end of this section in one piece. We breathed a sigh of relief, had a quick drink of water to relieve parched throats, and moved on over the much easier ground in front of us, even though it welcomed us with ankle-deep mud. The map showed that there were still some miles of rugged ground to cover before getting to Lamorna Cove.

Around about the midpoint to Lamorna, the thought stumbled into my mind that we had a problem; in fact, we had two problems. The sun still shone down from its fairly high angle, but it clearly didn't have too much farther to sink before evening came on. This route had always taken me the whole day to get into Penzance before nightfall. On this occasion, the mud had slowed us down just enough to make it doubtful that we could make it to Penzance, or the town of Newlyn, before dark. Even getting to the end of this wild section of path to reach the village of Mousehole by dark presented a problem this early in the year with the sun dipping restfully into the west by 8pm. The rougher sections of the coastal footpath are not very forgiving, and walking them after dark, or in fading light, could be pushing our luck.

The second problem concerned Brian. I knew that he had tried several times to ring his wife, Brenda. You may recall that she would be waiting for him in Penzance with the intention of going out for dinner that evening to celebrate their wedding anniversary. Mobile phone signals are notoriously elusive whenever you are below the top of the cliff line on these paths, and this clearly didn't help Brian. I suggested to him that his best plan would be to leave our group when we reached Lamorna, walk up the hill from the coast to the pub, ask to use their landline if he still couldn't get a signal, call Brenda, and ask her to whisk him the relatively short journey by road back to Penzance. He agreed that this sounded like a good plan. Then we had a group Eureka moment!

In view of the gradually fading light from the sun, and the unlikelihood of reaching Mousehole by dark, we could all go up to the pub in Lamorna, have a well-earned meal and a drink or two, then call for a minicab to take the remaining six of us back to Penzance to pick up the cars. This idea impressed and thrilled everyone, as you might imagine, and the proposal passed unanimously.

This put new life into us all, and our pace reflected that admirably. We reached Lamorna in good shape but were beginning to feel that we had been stretched generously for several hours. Ten minutes later, we reached the pub at the top of the hill. All of us were red in the face and breathing like vintage steam engines; that hill doesn't take any prisoners. What a finish to the two days of walking!

The time showed 7pm, but the notice on the pub door showed an opening time of 7.30pm. Taking off our muddy gaiters and boots helped to fill in the time, and sitting outside the pub at the tables was heavenly after the rigours of the day. Wood pigeons serenaded us against a background of 'screes' from swifts up above the trees, harvesting insects in the gathering twilight. Peace descended upon us all.

I spoke too soon. A group of Chinese visitors arrived by minibus to join the thirsty customers waiting for the pub to open. Richard loped off to get closer to the pub door, which opened just as he reached it. The visitors from the Orient had the same intention as Richard, but he beat them to the only table inside that was just big enough for our group or theirs. I've got to give it to Richard. He is charming, a strategic thinker, good-looking, and exudes charisma… we are so much alike!

The area around our table soon took on the appearance of a squatter camp. Boots, gaiters, anoraks, and rucksacks lodged in every available space, but at least our group had reached the end of the rainbow. We had comfortable seats, and the bar area started filling up with interesting locals who looked as if they might break into Cornish songs as the evening proceeded. Undoubtedly, Richard would then give us another rendering of his favourite sea shanties.

A waitress took our meal orders, and three of us hurried to the bar to order the drinks for our group. Brian came back from the bar beaming with relief. He managed to make contact with his wife on the landline, and although it was later than anticipated, Brenda took it philosophically. She would be with us to collect Brian in about fifteen to twenty minutes, and the two of them would hurtle back to Penzance in the car for their anniversary meal; that was a relief and a happy ending to the problem.

I looked around the table at the jollity of our group. Was it worth giving up my lone training walk to experience all of this? The answer was a definite 'yes'. Group walking would not suit me most of the time because I like the quietness and sustained thinking that comes with lone trekking, but this had been a refreshing and memorable walk. Previous friendships had been consolidated and strengthened, and new understandings emerged in unexpected ways. Dave proposed a toast to the success of the trip, and we all drank heartily to that.

I reflected back over the last two days to assess how good the walk had been from the point of view of training for my Kilimanjaro trip in September. Certainly, there were strengths and weaknesses in my hill-climbing endurance, and I knew the sort of exercises to work on to be ready in about four weeks' time for the first of my training walks with Jon. That would be the walk starting at Minehead on the north Somerset coast. It is also the start of the 630-mile South West Coast Path, one of the world's great walking trails. Our walk on the first section of the path was estimated to take us about four days, and that would take us to Barnstaple in Devon where we would catch the train back to Exeter and then onto the main-line service back to Plymouth.

Brian's wife arrived at that moment to scoop him up and transport him back to Penzance for their anniversary dinner. We all offered our congratulations for their wedding anniversary and hoped to see them back at the gym during the following week.

The party atmosphere was still vibrant when we were given the news from the bar staff that our minibus had just arrived to take us back to the car park in Penzance. Bills were settled, and off we all went. Not only was the journey pleasant, but both of our cars were safe and sound where they had been left. Dave, Arthur, and I said our goodbyes to Karen, Pearl, and Richard. Everyone expressed their wish to do this again one day, and time will tell if that can ever be achieved; let's hope so.

The journey back to Plymouth hurtled along into the late evening, and after dropping Arthur off, Dave deposited me at the door of my house. A shower and a good night's sleep beckoned, but whether I would go to the gym the next day didn't seem too likely at this stage. I found out later in the week that Pearl was the only one of our group to get to the gym the following morning. Admittedly, she lives very near the gym, but it was still a magnificent effort.

Richard, after an injury-free two days on the very rough terrain of the coastal footpath, was frolicking out in his garden the following morning, trying to entertain his dog after the two-day absence, when he lost his footing, fell over, and knocked himself about quite badly. Cuts, bruises, and grazes were abundant, but he is a hard guy to keep down and soon recovered enough to join us all again back at the gym.

Now, if you thought that was a good bit of training, wait until I tell you about my next session on the coastal footpath with Jon.

TEN

With about four weeks to wait until the next big walk, I started to formulate a gym and home-training plan to work on my weaknesses. The recent walk from St Ives to Penzance gave me some training areas to think about. In addition to these areas, I found myself being drawn powerfully back again to those books I had read about the experiences of other trekkers who had climbed Kilimanjaro and had lived to tell of their physical and mental punishment on this deceptive mountain.

With a sheet of A2 paper in front of me, I started to sketch out my first draft of the crucial areas to seriously work on. The more I engaged with this, the more daunting the task became. *Come on*, I ordered myself, *get your act together*. But my thoughts staggered onto the inevitable challenges waiting for me at my quite advanced age. Then, my adventurous self whispered to me that if I gave in now, it would hound me remorselessly until the day my quality trekking boots and Nordic walking poles were put on eBay, and I spent my days watching box sets of my favourite films and TV series and lounged around musing on what might have been and waiting to be called to life's 'departure lounge' for the biggest leap into the unknown that I could imagine. No! I would be going to Africa, and I would do my best to climb Mount Kilimanjaro, no matter what lay in store for me. In any event, if I backed out now, Jon would be seething with indignation, and he does a good line in that. Talking of Jon, he wouldn't be back from London for another two to three weeks. We must arrange some local walks on the coastal footpath and Dartmoor when he came back to Plymouth. This would lift our spirits for the big four-day training walk from Minehead to Barnstaple in five weeks' time.

Getting onto the coast path is so easy for us. My house is only about a hundred metres from where we can join the path as it curls around the estuary of the River Plym, meandering its way down to join the River Tamar in the magnificent stretch of inshore water called Plymouth Sound. By following the path up the coast for 210.5 miles, we could reach Poole in Dorset which is the official end (or beginning) of the southern route along this world-famous trail. By taking the passenger ferry across the River Tamar to Cremyl, we could, if we so wished, walk down to Land's End, around the coast back to St Ives, and then right up the north coast to the start (or the end) of the 630-mile South West Coast Path at Minehead. That massive section of the walk from Plymouth to Minehead is probably about 419 miles over mind-blowing terrain with seascapes to die for.

For those walkers whose intrepidity knows no bounds, something is coming that will transform the walking opportunities in England to a massive extent. This path will open up the whole distance of the coast around England, a distance of 2800 miles (4500km). It will be the longest managed and signposted coastal path in the world. What a prospect! I wonder if Jon will talk me into having a go at it when I am in my eighties. Perhaps I could develop the Masaai mindset and be like their elders who sometimes set out on a two-hundred-mile trek without second thoughts when they are in their eighties. But all this is just fantasy on my part, isn't it? Anyway, let's get back to the training plan.

It seemed to me that I should put the main emphasis on the following:

- Cardiovascular training, to expand the working capacity of the heart and lungs
- Leg strengthening
- Core strength
- Breathing exercises
- Joint exercises
- Shoulders and upper body
- Back strengthening
- Endurance
- Diet
- Mental preparedness
- And plenty of walking
- (Jon, what had you got me into here?!)

The cardiovascular aspects of this training may – if I am lucky – give me a better chance of coping with the altitude effect as we get higher up the mountain. There is no guarantee of this. Some star athletes have hit trouble when getting up to the higher reaches of Kilimanjaro and have been evacuated because of the very real risk to their health and even to their lives. Conversely, some trekkers of quite average fitness have reached the summit without too much discomfort, although it seems unlikely that anyone could walk up and down again without considerable effort, unless they were mountain people with the right physiological make-up for the job. In any event, fitness in all those aspects of my training plan is recommended by people who know a lot about the physical demands on trekkers attempting this mountain. One writer reflecting about his trek up to the summit said that his seven months of intensive training stood him in good stead, but he definitely did not feel that he had overtrained. This guy was in his forties, so the message I must take from that is my training has to be rigorous; no ifs, no buts.

I sat down to focus in on the facilities available to me. In many ways, I was fortunate in the opportunities so close to home or within a seven-minute drive. The gym I attend is only a five-minute drive away, so the treadmills, cross trainers, and stepper machines are there when I need them. However, for cardiovascular workouts, it is generally thought better if this type of training can be done in the fresh air. Clearly, the gym equipment will be far more pleasant in bad weather. But what is on offer among the many classes at the gym is the Interval Conditioning class, and this comes highly recommended. I made a note to join this class and crossed my fingers that I wouldn't make a complete fool of myself by being left behind puffing and panting in the first few gruelling minutes of the forty-five-minute class.

The seven-minute drive I mentioned would get me to an area of Plymouth called Mount Batten. Huge views of Plymouth Sound, the passing boat traffic, seagulls, a massive arc of sky, and the salty breezes rolling in from the ever-changing sea (sometimes glinting, sometimes seething and threatening) give this place a special resonance. Its main feature is a long breakwater thrusting out into Plymouth Sound, and this offers a great place to do a little sprinting after a good warm-up to get the blood flowing around the system. Another playful feature of this area is a set of eighty-six steep steps; yes, you guessed it, this is ready-made for cardio work and endurance by running up and down these a few times. What a great way to warm up for that sprinting I was telling you about!

So, the cardio and endurance sides of the training plan look good. I contacted the gym to book in for Zoe's Interval Conditioning classes, and they were scheduled to start in a few days. That gave me a breathing space to start my training programme and hopefully boost up my fitness level to some extent before venturing into the rigours of the class.

Next on the list was leg-strengthening. Being a keen and regular walker, my legs were quite strong. But the demands of Kilimanjaro would clearly be of a different order of magnitude when it came to steep, intense, and prolonged trekking. I spoke to two of our gym instructors to get their advice on a programme of effective leg exercises, and they were extremely helpful. They wrote out the details of a sequence to follow and instructed me in the weights to use and the number of repetitions to go for.

An old favourite leg-strengthening exercise is the squat and lunge, carrying a pair of dumbbells.

I used eighteen kilogram dumbbells for the standing squats and seven to ten kilograms for the lunging version.

An extension of the weighted lunge is the walking lunge where you take a long pace forward as in the basic lunge, then as you come forward into the standing position, take another pace forward on the other leg. The weights can make this a really good exercise. There is no mistaking the effect on your leg muscles after a few minutes of this one.

Yet another good leg and knee joint exercise involves a large fitness ball. You place the ball in the middle of your back, and it is sandwiched there by a wall behind you. You then sink down on your knees as far as you can go comfortably, while letting the ball roll down with you, then roll back up again while still maintaining contact with the ball in its position behind you to complete one sequence. I usually try for thirty sequences of this exercise.

It should go without saying that if you have knee problems, or any other medical problems that may cause you a problem, you should consult a medical professional. In fact, you may wish to do this in any event if you have any doubts about starting a fitness programme like this.

There are many other good leg exercises out there, but because of the time factor, I stuck to the ones described here, and I never suffered from any aches or pains or even tiredness in my legs on either our bigger training walks or on the mountain trek itself.

Core strength, as any good sprinter will confirm, is at the heart of great performance. It also helps a lot when you are on a multi-day trek taking in numerous testing hills or trekking up a mountain. Essentially, core strength in this context gives you that body leverage to keep good walking form and pace, especially when carrying a full backpack with camping gear, food for a few days, extra clothing, and cooking utensils.

Breathing exercises always seem to be good things to do for keeping fit and healthy, but could they help me to overcome the effects of altitude on the breathing mechanism? It seems that at the summit of Kilimanjaro, which is at nearly six thousand metres, the oxygen in the atmosphere will be about half what it is at sea level. Combine this with the effort of climbing up the steep approaches near the summit, and the lungs will probably be screaming out for more oxygen at every step of the ascent.

I made enquiries about what training one could pursue to prepare for this prospect but drew a blank. There are training masks to restrict the quantity of breath you can inhale when training for certain sports, but the reviews available didn't hold out any hope that these masks could help me at the altitude in question. I decided not to pursue this idea.

I spoke to a keen yoga practitioner about this problem and was given some breathing exercises to work on. The effect after a few days of practice convinced me that they could help, so I continued with them right up to the present day and feel better for them. It would take too long to detail them here, but a search on Amazon or a similar platform for a book or DVD on yoga breathing will provide a great selection if you would like to pursue this practice.

A helpful thought fluttered into my mind about the benefits of deep breathing, and it was this. Many people tend to be quite shallow breathers most of the time, that is they don't as a matter of habit engage the diaphragm situated below the lungs. This is like a pair of bellows to boost the breath and the quantity of oxygen circulating in the system to provide a good level of energy. One huge incentive to work on really getting your inhalations right down to the diaphragm, where it will serve you well, is to reflect on the way singers and brass and woodwind players tend to live longer and healthier lives on average. The practice of singing and playing these instruments effectively relies on exactly this method of breathing right down into the diaphragm as a matter of habit. Having been an orchestral trombone player for many years, my breathing follows this method automatically. This could serve me well on Kilimanjaro when the altitude effect kicked in, and time would tell, but it could also be one of the reasons I have reached seventy-five with no apparent health problems so far. Yoga breathing also tends to concentrate on this method of breathing, and that is why it could be beneficial to anyone thinking of this or a similar climb.

Exercising the joints is another excellent area to work on. It is so common to see people come into the gym and rush onto the treadmill, or one of the other machines, without any apparent warm-up. This can play hell with joints over time. It is like getting into a vehicle, revving up from cold, and accelerating away down the road before the engine gets the proper amount of oil to lubricate the cylinders. The result is undue wear and tear on the engine and a shortening of its efficient working life.

Joints need lubricating as well. The lubricant in this case is synovial fluid, and this can and should be stimulated to do its work before the serious exercise of the day starts. I find that this is particularly the case with knee joints. I came across this exercise a few years ago in a newspaper, and the exercise has served me well ever since.

Start by standing with the feet together. Bend the knees down to about a half squat. Rotate the knee joints in the way you would if you were doing hip rotations, but keep the rotations at a steady pace to allow the fluid to move around into the parts of the knee joints where it is needed. I usually do thirty rotations in a clockwise direction, then thirty anticlockwise. This should get the knees ready for some serious workout routines. You could use this same basic approach with your hips, ankles, shoulders, elbows, and wrists. Fingers can all be flexed at the same time several times.

Shoulders and upper body can be taken care of with such exercises as pull-ups, either on a machine to assist you with counterweights or perhaps by using a pull-up bar fixed above a door frame, as long as it is safe. Again, with all of these exercises, you should be totally sure that you are not going to do more harm than good. If in doubt at all, check with your medical professional.

Endurance. This is where I took a leap of faith and joined the Interval Conditioning class. What an experience that was!

My face must have burned as I entered the fitness studio and saw what awaited me in there. Thirty pairs of eyes fixed on me as I walked through the door. Most of the women in the studio were in their late teens, twenty-somethings, thirty-somethings, and the veterans – from forty up to an estimated late fifties – formed a tiny minority. I expected to be among the oldest in the class, and I achieved that honour with a massive margin. What I hadn't expected was that I would be the only guy on the block.

The lady instructor came over for a pleasant chat. She wanted to know if I had anything wrong with me. I rapidly pondered about a possible answer to that question in view of my being there at all, but settled for a smug, 'nothing at all'. She seemed to be impressed and wrote something in her notebook… but it definitely wasn't my phone number.

The class got under way, and within a couple of minutes into the warm-up, I felt my lungs working like a steam train that rattles and wheezes its way up a mountainside. I hung in there, hoping fervently that the rattling sound in my upper chest wasn't a death rattle.

With the warm-up completed, we worked through a range of testing exercises for the next forty minutes of slow, demanding stuff, followed by fast, demanding stuff. The essence of interval training seared into my consciousness with the power of an epiphany. But this particular epiphany came with a painful payoff the following morning. Yes, it was hard, but I had been converted to the potential of interval training in a big way. I chatted with the other members of the group as the training sessions progressed over the next few weeks, and there was a lot of interest in my coming trek up

Kilimanjaro. I became so keen on interval training that I continued the sessions after the expedition had been completed. If you have never tried this form of training, I can thoroughly recommend it to you, always bearing in mind that you must make sure that your health and fitness are suited to the demands that it will put on your body. It makes sense to build up to this training incrementally, unless you are already very fit and active.

Diet is another significant factor in the training mix. I think that most people accept that certain types of food can potentially give you more energy and vitality, more health and zing than other types of food. It's easy to be discouraged by the way experts often disagree with one another about what benefits we can get from different food choices and balances within one's overall diet. So, what is the answer for each of us as individuals?

Pragmatic testing offers us a reasonable doorway to better health, and a good baseline from which to build our higher level of fitness. Our bodies seem to be capable of letting us know when we are functioning well. It's that feeling when we start the day with a higher level of enthusiasm. It is also that feeling carrying on into the way we set off for the day ahead, with a certain 'bounce'. Perhaps it's the noticeable way in which we are more open to challenges, and grasping opportunities that come along. We engage more with life. Days are where we live our lives, and we now seem to have the energy to make the most of each day as an adventure. But to get into that 'zone' we need self-discipline. As the saying goes, the body keeps a reckoning.

So, what are these foods that help us to enter this enticing zone? I study the healthy living tips in our daily papers for any special survey results from recognised authorities such as universities and other acknowledged experts in the field. If a particular food is vaunted as an ideal storehouse of certain nutrients, vitamins, and other desirable features, then I shortlist it for regular inclusion in my diet. I often do an online search to get an overview of other studies about this particular food and any reservations that eminent people in the field may have raised. Naturally, these reservations need to be backed up by some compelling facts or indicators.

I look for the ratio of good comments against those that are more off-putting. All being well, I find enough factual evidence to include the food in question for a trial period. Over time (perhaps a few weeks or months), I wait for my body to let me know if there has been any noticeable uplift in those factors mentioned above. Sometimes there will be something detectable, other times not; it needs patience and time to carry out a fair test.

Broccoli was the first food I tested in this way. I am now a firm fan of this vegetable, and I really do notice the difference in my stamina and general health. The way I include this into my diet is to chop the broccoli very small and have this raw on my daily salad which I eat slowly. My energy level is high in relation to many guys of my age that I know, and I often get the feeling that I am like a tightly coiled spring as I launch that stored energy into whatever the day is going to be about; like a space vehicle forcing it's acceleration up through the atmosphere's increasing resistance until it reaches escape velocity and breaks free of gravity's manacles as it punches out into space!

Another highly recommended food is nuts. Peanuts are very high in protein and therefore excellent for snacks when training hard. Your protein needs to be boosted after your body is stretched during a workout.

Walnuts are also generously beneficial. These nuts are full of nutrients. The big surprise with walnuts is that they are extremely good for brain health, especially as we get older. They can also boost the brain's sharpness and memory power.

Nut butters are another good source of the wide range of nutrients that nuts possess. It is often easy to see the oil from the nuts when they are in butter form. This oil, far from being fattening, is a great source of the oil the body needs as part of a healthy diet and, in sensible amounts, doesn't appear to be a risk to putting on weight.

Complex carbohydrates like sweet potatoes are also highly recommended, as are lean meats like turkey and chicken breast. Green, leafy vegetables score high up in the food scale, as does extra virgin olive oil for adding to salads. To get plenty of dietary fibre, I searched the bread shelves in our supermarkets for loaves with higher-than-average fibre content. It seems that a ratio somewhere in the region of five to one for carbohydrates in relation to fibre in bread is recommended, but in my experience, that balance can be difficult to find. Perseverance is the name of the game.

In order to get my weight down to the ideal level, I adopted the semi-fasting method. This works by only eating between, say, 7am and 7pm each day, unless there is a very good reason to break out of that pattern. The twelve hours of fasting through the late evening to breakfast time allows the body to deal efficiently with the sensible amount of food consumed during the day. Adjusting to this new routine was a little strange to start with, but it soon became a habit with me, and people started to comment on how well I was looking. At the same time, I was feeling lighter and more energetic. Even my consumption of sugary foods tailed off considerably. My alcohol consumption has always been low, and that has stayed constant at about four to five medium glasses of red wine a week. But my water consumption has risen to about five or six average-sized glasses a day. Water intake is vitally important when trekking up high mountains as this helps to counter the effect of altitude sickness. And talking about mountains and training, Jon was now back from London, and we would be setting out the next day for the first of our big training walks. Join us then for some dramatic surprises.

ELEVEN

The day was here at last. We met up at the train station at 7am on a beautifully sunny morning that beamed with promise. I hadn't travelled by train for several years, and there were strange surprises waiting for me.

To start with, Jon had to do battle with the digital ticket machine for five minutes before it became obvious that the thing was out of order but in a misleading way. Luckily, we found another two machines nearby that were working. I had never had to use machines to buy train tickets before, and I wondered what would have happened had there been difficulty with the other two machines as well. The ticket desk had just opened and already had a queue of several passengers waiting to buy tickets for their journeys. Our train would be leaving in ten minutes, so the new world (to me) of machines and minimal staff to maximise railroad profits could have been a real problem for us. Jon, being used to travelling into London from Reading every working day, seemed well-versed in the problems of using the trains in this new modern age.

We boarded our train for Taunton and found a couple of seats in a fairly restricted corner of the first compartment we entered. I glanced at our fellow passengers and noticed a certain aura of complacent acceptance on the faces of several of them. But when

Jon explained to me that this train was going all the way to Glasgow, several hundred miles up the line, I found it difficult to believe that the rail company could get away with such cramped and basic comfort for passengers travelling all that way or even half that distance. The carriages seemed more suited to a branch line taking passengers for just a few miles up the track. Is it just me, or are there certain aspects of modern life that have bypassed the consideration of the general public or even common decency? Jon looked at me condescendingly as I droned on about such matters. He was clearly used to these facts of life and probably thought that at least we had seats to be thankful for. I realised that there was nothing to be done about the level of comfort so changed my conversation to send out waves of optimism about the four great days of trekking that lay ahead of us. Jon told me again how much he was buzzing about this first of the three trips that would take us eventually right down the coastal path to our destination, Penzance.

Within about fifteen minutes of arriving at Taunton, I decided to visit the on-board toilet facilities. Well, what a surprise that was! Being a 'hick from the sticks', I had no idea how so much had changed with rail travel. First of all, the doorway to the toilet was curved instead of the traditional flat surface. This completely confused me, and I spent several moments wandering around trying to find the toilet. When the penny finally dropped, and I realised that the curved surface really was the toilet door, I pressed the button to open the door and shocked a lady occupant who had presumably forgotten to lock the door. She apologised; I apologised, and everything then seemed all right again with the world, until I saw another array of press-buttons inside the toilet. The least apparent of these was the button to press to lock the door. I found myself wondering what would happen if that button went out of order in the locked position. How could one escape? With a bit of luck, this would be my sternest challenge of the day. Unfortunately, there was a sterner challenge to come later in the morning.

I arrived back at the seat to find Jon looking perturbed at my absence. Having explained to him all about my adventures with modern train technology, he was more convinced than ever that I should not be allowed out by myself into the modern world. Obviously, he was joking… wasn't he? Anyway, that was quickly forgotten because the train then pulled into Taunton station.

The next part of the journey was to Minehead, the start of the South West Coast Path. We had the choice of going out to the coast by steam train or by the bus service. The steam train sounded like fun until we checked out the price. The bus service was definitely the top favourite, and there just outside the station the Minehead bus was waiting. I boarded the bus first and produced my senior citizens bus pass for a free ride. Jon's face winced with indignation when he was charged three or four pounds. He knew that this could be the start of many similar experiences if we needed to use buses on certain days to cut our journey times down in order to reach our overnight accommodation at a reasonable time in the evening. I tried to commiserate with him, but this seemed to deepen the wounds of his theatrical indignation.

The journey to Minehead proved to be scenic and enjoyable, and this soon took his mind off the injustice he had suffered over having to pay the bus fare. I also gave him one of my favourite chocolate bars as a consolation.

* * *

Walking through the town towards the seafront, the tangy, salty, seaweedy smells floated up the main street, carried along by the light breezes coming off the Bristol Channel. What a great start to our first day's walk! Jon had been anticipating this day for weeks, and I was overjoyed to see his face brighten and lighten after his last-but-one tour of duty in London. Three days in early September would be the final call on his service with the Metropolitan Police. This last duty call would be to monitor criminal activity at the Notting Hill Carnival. Just a few days after that, we would be flying to Tanzania to climb Kilimanjaro; there must surely be worse ways to start one's retirement.

We reached the seafront and jostled our way through the holidaymakers licking their lavish ice creams and eating their post-breakfast burgers as they enjoyed the day. It didn't take long for us to reach the monument that marks the start (or the finish) of the 630 miles of coastal footpath that winds its way down the Somerset coast, the North Devon coast, then the Cornish coast, the South Devon coast, and finally the Dorset coast to finish at Poole. We only have our sights set on a total of 230 miles, spread over the three separate training sessions, to get us finally to Penzance, and we have our fingers crossed for good weather. This is a picture of Jon gazing admiringly at the monument with its giant hands coming up out of the pavement and holding the Ordnance Survey map of the way ahead:

Jon at the start of our journey in Minehead, looking at the monument that signifies the beginning of the South West Coast Path

On we walked along the pavements and road for several hundred yards until we reached a small park. There was a waymark sign pointing our route into the park, and we could see that at the end of the park, the real start of the path began with a hill climb into a towering woodland. There happened to be a convenient sheltered seating area just before the take-off point, so we decided to rearrange our rucksacks so that everything we might need could be reached with ease.

It was at this point that Jon's mobile phone rang out. "Sorry, mate, but it's the wife calling. I'd better take it. Sue probably wants to wish us luck as she knows that we are starting out on the trip this morning."

"No problem, Jon. I'll just check out a few things on the map."

"I'm really sorry to hear that, Sue… it sounds really bad… how long has he been in hospital? How is your mum taking it? Listen, I will explain everything to Eric and head straight back to Minehead to pick up a bus to Taunton and then back to Reading by train. I should be with you sometime in the early evening… no, I insist. With your father being that ill, it is the least I can do… no, Sue, it is something I feel I ought to do. He has been very good to me over the years… all right, I will wait to hear from you after you have talked it over with your mum, but I am ready to shoot back home at a moment's notice… right, let me know as soon as you can… yes, I will explain it all to Eric and he will understand… love you, darling… bye now."

Jon's face saddened into a look of deep concern as he explained the situation to me. I knew how much he wanted to get on with this training walk, and my heart went out to him. The timing of all this was cruel, but it wasn't anyone's fault. It felt like fate testing us, and I knew that we were far from beaten.

It was agreed that if he went back to Reading, I would carry on with the trek to Barnstaple. Jon knew the itinerary, and we could see that the further I was from Minehead, and our first overnight stop at Porlock, the less chance there would be for him to find me again even if he didn't need to stay long at Reading and the London hospital where his father-in-law was in a critical condition. Jon's best hope would be that he could join me on the second part of the trek in about five weeks' time when we would be trekking from Barnstaple to Newquay in Cornwall.

I talked with Jon about his immediate plan. Clearly, he wouldn't find it exhilarating just hanging about Minehead waiting for the call from Sue. He accepted that he could improve on that by walking with me to our overnight stop at Porlock, about eight miles away. There was a regular bus service from Porlock back to Minehead, and there could even be a service straight back to Taunton. There was also the possibility that Jon may not be needed to travel back home at this point, in which case he would be able to carry on with our walk tomorrow until such times as he might be asked to travel home. That plan seemed the best in the circumstances, and we strode out to scale our first hill of the day.

The coolness of the woodland baffled the sun's overplayful attempt to welcome us to the coastal footpath. Our upwards path eventually came out onto an open ridge with striking views across the Bristol Channel, with the Welsh coast in the far distance. Larks sang to lift our spirits, and the going was easy along a well-trodden pathway. I reflected on Jon's awkward situation in not knowing from one minute to the next if he would need to abandon this fine walk in such good weather conditions. All we could do was press on and hope that Jon's father-in-law's illness wasn't life-threatening.

After about two hours of walking, we stood on a rocky promontory looking down into the amazing scenery of Porlock Vale far below. I pointed out to Jon where we would be staying that night, and it was clear that we had plenty of time to relax and enjoy the surroundings on this first, and easiest, day of the four-day trek:

Jon on the heights above Porlock Vale, with part of the following day's walk stretching out behind him.

At this point, I had a good idea. I remembered that there was an attractive tea garden down in the Vale, situated just where our route took us off the hills and into meadow country. The tea garden is in the pleasant hamlet of Bossington where the cottage gardens produce the tallest hollyhocks I have ever seen. This place is ready-made for a couple of dehydrated travellers with some uncertainty hovering over them, and I knew that Jon could do with some cheering up.

The birdsong and garden fragrances lifted our mood as soon as we walked into the garden. There weren't many customers in the garden at that stage, and we found a table favoured with a border of flowers dancing with the light breezes in a way that the poet Wordsworth would have found oddly reminiscent, and it seems likely that Wordsworth, and his friend Coleridge, would have passed through Bossington on their extensive walking trips when they lived for a year in the local area of Nether Stowey. Tea being ordered, we relaxed into this lovely setting and counted our blessings.

With the tea and cakes came the sparrows and robins to try to convince us that they were starving. I looked at Jon and wondered just how different all this must be to working for thirty pressurised years in London. My great hope was that he would be able to carry on with this walk after today, and I resolved to make this experience as good as I could for him, given the present circumstances. We agreed that tea gardens were good for us, and, where possible, we would seek them out on our treks over the next three months, as long as we were keeping to schedule.

We eventually dragged ourselves away from this rural idyll and headed over the lark-happy meadows towards the little town of Porlock. The afternoon had progressed quite a bit, and we looked forward to getting into the guest house, unpacking, having a shower, and perhaps a look around the small town to choose a pub for the evening meal. I hadn't visited Porlock for two or three years, so it was pleasant to think back on those previous trips.

We arrived at the guest house and were greeted warmly by our host, David, and his Labrador, Archie. Once we were cleaned up and settled, I asked Jon if he would like another excellent, but easy, walk up through Hawkcombe Woods. It is a walk of no more than about three miles on a decent track through fir trees on one side and deciduous trees on the other. This is set off by a chuckling brook that runs through the centre of the woodland all the way down to Porlock; in fact, we would be following it up from the town, past an old watermill and several attractive flower-adorned cottages. Jon loved the idea, so on went the walking boots again, and off we went.

Jon was instantly taken by the beauty of this cool walk after the exploits of the earlier part of the day's walking in hot weather. Off we ambled to sharpen our appetites for the evening meal in the very old Ship Inn.

We arrived at the Ship after our walk through the woods, and we were ready for that meal. The Ship is so atmospheric that you can feel its history seeping out of the stonework and timbers. The poet Coleridge stayed here at least once, and the Inn competes with at least two other local locations as the place where Coleridge drifted in an opium dream during which he conceived the famous poem of *Kubla Khan*.

Another famous event took place just outside the Ship Inn. Back in the year 1899, a sailing ship was in danger of being overwhelmed by the waves off Porlock. The nearest lifeboat was at Lynmouth about thirteen miles down the coast. But due to the fierce wind, and its direction, the lifeboat could not be launched from its home port. Someone came up with the challenging idea that the ten-ton lifeboat should be taken overland to Porlock Weir, near Porlock, where it could be possible to launch. If you know the hills between Lynmouth and Porlock, you would be horrified at the prospect of hauling a heavy wooden boat over that terrain, especially in those days when the roads were much rougher than they are today.

Teams of horses and men were assembled to tow the lifeboat, and off they set to the challenging first hill leading from Lynmouth up to the high ridge, leading eventually to Porlock. Going up such hills must have been Homeric, but what awaited them on the route down into Porlock was terrifying. It is, even in these days, one of the most notorious hills in England. It is not just its steepness of twenty-five per cent, but its twisting and turning nature with hairpin-tight bends. At the bottom of the hill these days, it is common to smell burning brake linings from vehicles as drivers struggle to keep the speed down to a controllable level, even in low gear. This is the steepest of any A-road in the whole of the UK.

The horse-drawn wagon must have been hellish to control on Porlock Hill. But, in the end, it was managed, at least until the final section just outside the Ship Inn was reached. It was not possible to get the wagon between two buildings on opposite sides of the road. What could be done? Mariners' lives were at stake. There was only one way around it – part of the cottage on one side of the road had to be demolished as quickly as possible.

It was untimely that just after demolition work had taken place, a message reached the lifeboat crew and all their helpers that the ship that had been in danger was now apparently safe. But what a great effort! The story has lived on in the local area, and further afield, even after all this time. I wonder if the Ship Inn played host to all those thirsty pullers and pushers on that day, and that's what you call a silly speculation!

We ambled back to the guest house after the meal. Our route took us past Porlock's historic church. I told Jon about its association with King Arthur and Queen Guinevere. The church is dedicated to Saint Dubricius, the very saint who reputedly married the royal couple. Jon looked sceptically at me, but I reassured him that the story is recorded in the town's historical records. Perhaps it is Jon's years as a detective, but he still could not accept this story at face value; some people are like that, I suppose.

We had a good night's sleep. As we were just getting ready to go down to breakfast, Jon's mobile phone lacerated into our optimism for the day ahead. It was Sue, but the report was fortunately neutral. Ken's condition had not deteriorated during the night. Jon again offered to return home immediately, but Sue thought it better to await events, and she would keep in touch with Jon during the day. Jon explained that it would not always be possible to get a signal on the coast path between Porlock and Barnstaple, so a text might be necessary as the default option. In any event, Jon would keep in touch periodically when a signal became available.

So far, so good; the prospects for some trek training that day looked reasonable. All we needed now was some breakfast. I hadn't told Jon just how good David's breakfasts were; that would be a surprise. Jon has a reputation for being a big eater, especially when he is doing a lot of outdoor exercise. I often blame his huge need for food on what I can only assume to be the giant tapeworm clamouring for calories in his stomach. Let's see if Jon still looks hungry after David's lavish spread.

As predicted, the breakfast overwhelmed us. Jon did his best to eat everything is sight, and it was a stunning effort. Luck came to help us in the shape of Archie, the Labrador. Archie, being a bit sneaky, waited for David to be occupied on some household chores. This was Archie's chance. He nipped into the dining room and settled for a pork sausage and scrambled egg; I think it is called 'native cunning'.

Having had a splendid breakfast to give us energy for the day, we grabbed our gear, settled the bill with David, said our goodbyes to Archie – who looked well pleased with these two particular pilgrims – and hit the trail.

TWELVE

We picked up a woodland path on the edge of the town. This path is more attractive than the actual coast path between Porlock and Porlock Weir, and not being purists, it suited us on this occasion. It wouldn't be the only detour on this day, but more of that surprising adventure later.

Porlock Weir was quiet at this time in the morning, but one or two businesses were just opening. A tiny fish and chip shop opened as we passed, and the owner tried to sell us some of what he called the finest chips in the West Country. I declined the offer. Jon's nostrils were twitching as the smell of freshly cooked fish and chips wafted out into the post-breakfast world.

"That was a great breakfast at David's an hour ago," I mumbled, as if talking to myself.

It had the right effect, and Jon wrestled with the devil worm and beat him… on this occasion.

The route from Porlock Weir becomes steep soon after leaving the coastline. Up we climbed into impressive woodland. Many of the trees are old and bearded with skeins of green, matted, beard-like vegetation. The path is good, and it eventually delivered us to Culbone Church. This is reputedly the smallest parish church in England. It sits in its little clearing by a sweet-sounding brook with birdsong chiming into the ancient silences that pervade this lovely spot.

Jon sat on a garden bench to study our map, and I saw the potential for a photograph; click, and it was done before Jon realised that I had immortalised him in electronic media:

Deep in the coastal woodland at the tiny and remote church of Culbone; a serene setting

This place is so tranquil that we only moved on with reluctance. There was more hill-climbing ahead of us up through the woodland initially, then out onto more open terrain along a good path with an increasing number of hedges. We came to a gate in the hedge on our right and viewed a strange sight. There was a huge white mass below us where the Bristol Channel should have been. This sea mist lay rolled out in front of us for as far as the eye could see. It was like being in an aircraft looking down on the cloud layer below. We were still in the glorious sunshine up at our height, but it seemed unlikely that any sunlight could have filtered its beams down through that blanket of cotton wool. We didn't see anything like that again until the morning of our second day on Kilimanjaro. But on that day, we saw the distant summit of Mount Meru jutting up through the sparkling cloud layer, quite a sight!

It was at this point that there came another call from Sue. Everything was still unchanged at the hospital. Jon could still carry on with the walk at this stage.

I discussed the alternative that lay open for us if we would like a change from coastal walking. We could cut across a couple of fields, along the Porlock to Lynmouth road for a while, then down into the valley that would take us to The Stag Hunter's Inn at the village of Brendon.

"There will still be plenty of walking to do from Brendon down the river to Lynmouth, but we could stop for a drink in the Stag Hunter's for a quick rest after all the walking we've done in the past four hours," I coaxed.

Jon went for the idea without any hesitation, so we branched off to the left, away from the coast for a while, and set out on our new course. We reached Brendon after about forty-five minutes. The river garden of the Inn was completely empty of customers, so we chose a sunny seat by the river. Jon went into the bar to get our drinks. Just as he disappeared into the doorway of the Inn, I saw a flash of stunning colour a few feet away over the river. What a great surprise – it was a kingfisher in all its sumptuous glory! Jon would be devastated to have missed that sight, so I decided not to tell him and avoid spoiling this lovely afternoon for him.

There we sat in the radiance, with Jon enjoying his pint of cider and me staring at the trickles of condensation moving snail-like down my glass of 'Proper Job'. It was reminiscent of the scene in *Ice Cold in Alex* when the four travellers sat in the cool bar, stared at the ice-cold drinks in front of them, and reflected briefly on their narrow escapes from the desert, before downing those beers at lightning speed. Jon's face opened into astonishment as I uncharacteristically drank my pint of 'Proper Job' at Mach speed.

"Ready for another, Jon?"

He knew that I was not a great beer drinker, so my performance with that pint was like something out of *Tales of the Unexpected*.

I came back with the round of drinks, and there followed another of those 'unexpected' tales.

Jon asked me if I knew that he was going through a very difficult time at home with Sue and the four daughters. I had no idea about him having any problems like that. He told me the sad story of the tightrope the marriage was teetering on, and I felt deeply sorry for him and the family, especially right at the beginning of his retirement. It was clear that Jon's father-in-law's illness may bring the family back together again. Jon was certainly willing to travel back home at a moment's notice, and this could help the situation. I would do whatever I could to help him in this difficult period of his life.

We sat and talked about more cheerful things until the sun started to lose some of its heat – time to hit the trail if we wanted to get to Lynmouth before nightfall. We left the Inn feeling a little the worse for wear. Staggering slightly, I led the way back over Brendon Bridge so that we could get onto the long river walk through the woods and down to Lynmouth.

I hoped that Jon would enjoy this walk, and he did. My own cherished memories of the first time I walked along this river in 2001 with Judith and our two Labradors was as clear to me as if it were only yesterday. Jon also fell instantly in love with this delightful river valley, as I had hoped. He needed to feel the healing power of nature, particularly at this time in his life.

After a while, we came to the tiny riverside hamlet of Rockford. I told Jon about a strange experience that happened to me there when staying with Judith and our two Labradors in one of the river cottages. We had been out walking for the whole morning and part of the afternoon before arriving back at the cottage. As we entered the cottage, a powerful feeling came over me that I had to turn on the television. It was as if something was compelling me, and I had no choice in the matter. As the first pictures flashed onto the screen, we thought we were watching a film. A jet was shown crashing into a huge skyscraper. Then, we heard an announcer's voice say in total shock that a second plane had also crashed in an identical way.

We were both as stunned as the announcer. It was a moment we will never forget. It was 9/11, and the year was 2001. What had so powerfully compelled me to go to the television, I could not say. It felt like being caught up in a wave of energy that may have been pulsing around the world. The strangeness of that compelling power still sometimes echoes in my mind twenty years on.

* * *

We walked into Lynmouth as twilight soothed the western sky with its rose light. The walk had been just as wonderful as my memory of the first time I had travelled down that route. What is more, Jon had clearly enjoyed it as well. All we had to do now was find the Airbnb accommodation and get a good night's sleep ready for the big section that would take us to Ilfracombe tomorrow.

Finding that accommodation was like trying to fathom out a way to do the Rubik's Cube puzzle. The address we had didn't seem to make sense. We quickly came to the conclusion that we may have been conned. As a last resort, we went into a small pub to ask any likely looking locals if they could help us to find the house. We found two locals who claimed that they had never heard of the place. This could be our first night of sleeping in a bus shelter or perhaps a hedge… hope it didn't rain!

We decided on one last look around the narrow streets in the general area that Jon had been given in the owner's instructions. We found it. The cottage door was hiding behind a large shrub, and we must have walked past it three or four times before actually seeing it.

And the next problem pounced on us straight away. The instruction from the owner said that there was a key box by the door, but there didn't appear to be any box. I brushed away some vegetation and uncovered some sort of box near ground level. It looked like an old electrical junction box. Jon tried to get the cover off the thing just in case it was the key box, but we were not hopeful. The cover did not budge. It seemed that we were destined to sleep outdoors that night after all.

Then along came the cavalry in the shape of a fellow walker who hailed from South Africa. He asked if he could help as he had had a lot of experience with similar problems. It was just as he moved in to have a look at the box that Jon suddenly realised that instead of opening outwards as a door would, this one just happened to open like an up-and-over garage door in miniature. Bingo! We could now enter the code that the owner had given us. With fingers crossed for good luck, but with our recent knowledge that if it could go wrong, it would go wrong, Jon entered the code… nothing. *That's it*, I thought. *We might as well accept that we will be sleeping out under the stars tonight.* But no… it was tricky to see the keypad properly with it being so close to ground level, and Jon had punched in at least one incorrect digit. Our South African friend had a torch handy, and with this to help him, Jon managed to enter the code and get the key from its compartment.

The accommodation made up for all the problems. It was clean and tidy and had a great view of the harbour in all its late evening splendour. We only unpacked the minimum amount of gear in order to get away early the following morning. Getting to sleep didn't present a problem, and we were both up with the seagulls just as dawn stretched and yawned its way into the new day and the challenges awaiting us. It was at this point that we realised that we had forgotten to have an evening meal; the beer back at The Stag Hunter pub really was stronger than we appreciated.

Cereal with powdered milk, and coffee, were the only items on the menu for breakfast, so we hoped to find somewhere in the town of Lynton at the top of the cliffs where we could replenish our supplies and perhaps find an early opening cafe for a good breakfast. Lynmouth itself doesn't appear to have any grocery stores or mini-markets, so local shopping is done up the steep cliff climb to Lynton; perhaps this is why the locals generally look quite fit.

We set off for Lynton before there were many signs of life in Lynmouth. There is an impressive rack and pinion railway to take passengers up the cliff to Lynton, but it didn't start its service until around mid-morning; far too late for us. That left us with the option of the steep cliff path up through trees and shrubs, augmented by some good views. Whoever decided on the route of the path when it was being developed into its present form did an excellent job. It zigzags its way up the cliff in a way that doesn't leave the average walker completely exhausted by the time the top is reached. But it did leave us with that empty feeling one gets shortly after a sparse breakfast. Jon was particularly listless this morning. He had that calorie-deficient, haunted look about him, and I surmised that his tapeworm had started to cut up a bit nasty. Would we be lucky enough to find a food shop or the oasis of a cafe open at just before 8am? I hoped so, for Jon's sake. His tapeworm could even be an alien form as in the film of the same name.

Luck happened to be on our side this day, so far. There was a mini-market in the main street as we walked into Lynton, and it was open. We restocked with snacks and bottled water for our journey to Ilfracombe, a long day's march away. Our questions about any likely place in the town that might just be open for breakfast met with the anticipated reply. We did another circuit around the store and chose some fruit, chocolate and the odd cake to stand in for breakfast. All we needed now was a convenient place to sit down to have our breakfast before hitting the coast trail once again.

As we entered the store, the sky was grey and sullen. On leaving the store, the threatening sky poured down its derision upon us. Oh well, that's backpacking for you! The rain splattered down steadily and sulkily but not viciously. What the hell, we were stoics, weren't we? We would certainly need to be stoics if this weather continued all the way to Penzance over the next three months. We had put on our Gore-Tex anoraks and waterproof trousers, so things could have been a lot worse without the proper gear for the job. In any event, we would need to be resilient to climb Kilimanjaro, and we reminded ourselves that this trek that we were on now was intended to be a training walk to help get us up that mountain.

Just as we were leaving Lynton, a small, deserted sports field appeared. We decided to investigate and went through an archway into the grounds. There, in front of us, just happened to be a small wooden gazebo. Jon's face brightened into hope, and we decided instantly that this presented a perfect place to stop for breakfast. We soon whipped through our ad hoc meal. Just as we were packing up to leave, I spotted a pile of change on the seat beside me. It amounted to nearly four pounds, and I gave it a new home in my purse. Jon, of course, called me all the lucky devils under the sun.

On we walked to pick up the coast path again at The Valley of the Rocks. The strange rocky outcrops and upthrusts are striking reminders of what geology can surprise us with. As we were gazing at these features, the wild goats that this valley is famous for put in an appearance through the curtains of mist that swirled around. It was a sight to remember.

The rain had stayed with us all the way from Lynton, but after a while it ceased to be a hindrance; in fact, some walkers claim to prefer walking in wet conditions because it tends to be a lot quieter as the human traffic drops right off. We hadn't seen any other walkers since leaving Lynton, and this area is usually extremely popular.

The impressive Torr Abbey appeared as we travelled on, and even from a distance it has a peaceful quality about it. I can understand why retreats are so sought-after in this abbey.

Dropping down the hillside from the abbey, an attractive cottage tea garden came into view. The sign outside told us that it would open at 10.30am, and it was now only 10am; what a pity. I suddenly spotted some movement in the cottage, and a young lady appeared on the balcony to lay a table. I shouted over the length of the long garden to ask if she would consider making two 'pilgrims' a pot of tea and perhaps a toasted teacake, if there were any at this time in the morning. She checked with the lady in charge, and we were granted a pre-opening concession. There were four jolly ladies on the staff that morning, and they sat down at the table next to ours on the covered balcony to have a quiet cuppa before the customers started turning up. It was clearly a popular venue. I could see that, even in the rain, this cottage garden had plenty of charm. The birds certainly liked this place. Looking beyond the garden, I could see the abbey in all its meditative glory, cresting the hill that we had just descended.

We hit the trail again and went straight into a long hill climb. There would be many hills today, but this one wasn't on the coast path. Our accommodation that night waited for us in Ilfracombe, several hilly miles away. This meant that some shortcuts needed to be taken if we were to get to Ilfracombe in good time for an evening meal. By looking seawards, I could see the actual coast path far below us with its background of petulant waves thrashing into the coastline with great plumes of spray. We had chosen a good alternative route that would save us useful time and energy for what lay waiting for us over the next seven hours.

The top of this long and demanding hill at last came into view, and shortly after this, we found a scenic bridleway that eventually led us to a good pub called the Hunter's Inn where we could get a decent lunch to make up for the strange breakfast we had in the rain-lashed gazebo at Lynton.

The rain stopped shortly after lunch, and we started hitting steep and remorseless hill climbs on our way to Combe Martin. These hills were what we came for, and they proved one thing: Jon had the steady stamina to plod up the steep slopes like a machine on auto-climb. I, on the other hand, put in a pretty good effort but always dragged a little way behind Jon on the biggest climbs. It was probably better not to push myself too far, just find my comfortable pace and take the occasional short breather. One thing I did find out was that my recovery rate happened to be quite fast, and this could be a bonus on Kilimanjaro. Kilimanjaro should be relatively easy after these hills; at least, that was what Jon said, although rather unconvincingly.

Combe Martin came into view towards the end of the afternoon. This is an interesting and atmospheric place that I should like to explore some day when there might be more time available. But time now featured large in our planning. I pored over the map to assess whether we could manage the walk to Ilfracombe and get there in good time to find our Airbnb accommodation, plus find a place for our evening meal.

The coast path to Ilfracombe looked about seven miles over typical hilly and rough terrain. I spotted a fine-looking campsite on the map about halfway along the route; what a pity we weren't camping on this trip. We discussed the situation and decided to take advantage of the bus service to Ilfracombe. The bus arrived just as we decided on our plan, so, on we jumped. Guess what? Jon was aghast and appalled when I managed to get another free ride by producing my senior citizen's bus pass. Why could he not just rejoice at my good fortune?

We reached Ilfracombe in good time to get sorted out for the evening. The owner of the bnb lived on-site, so there were no access problems this time. This lady told Jon at the booking stage that she provided an opulent breakfast, and we were looking forward to starting the following morning with a really good meal to get our day off to a splendid start. In fact, we had been looking forward to that opulent breakfast throughout the day's march. But things do not always work out the way we expect.

The friendly landlady led us up to the third-floor bedroom. Jon asked her where the dining room was and the time of breakfast. The lady looked taken aback.

"Breakfast will be in your room, and I have wrapped it up and put it behind the bedroom door."

Jon's face wrinkled into dry riverbeds of unaccustomed creases. I reflected on how this started to show his age. My expectations were more moderate, and when Jon looked at me in sheer disbelief and disappointment, I had to pinch myself to keep my laughter suppressed.

We had reached the room. Behind the door, there was a neatly arranged tray with carefully wrapped bread, cheese, fruit, and marmalade. There were coffee and tea-making facilities. I was sure that this would keep us going on another tough walk on the following day. Jon said nothing, but his face was *opulently* expressive.

Jon went into a rant when the lady left us to it, and I couldn't help laughing at the way our expectations were shocked into acceptance of the reality of it all. Jon finally abandoned his indignation, smiled faintly, then permitted a broad grin to spread stoically across his tanned face. We agreed that Airbnb hadn't so far turned us into enthusiasts. I reminded Jon that we only had two more of these Airbnbs booked in, and the first one was for the first night on our second training walk in a little over two weeks' time. The final bnb would be in the surfing epicentre of Devon, the town of Bude. The accommodation for the remaining nights was booked into youth hostels. I had stayed at two hostels before in my early days as a backpacker, and I was intrigued to know what Jon would make of their typical spartan simplicity. For my money, wild camping, or even using campsites, would definitely be my preference unless the weather on a trip turned nasty.

*　*　*

Ilfracombe's nightlife that evening tended to be on the quiet side. We walked around the mainly empty lanes down near the harbour and kept our eyes open for any appealing pub where we could get a meal and a nice pint of real ale.

Jon agreed that we should have a look at the controversial statue on the harbour wall. The statue in question is Damien Hirst's 'Verity'. We rounded a bend at the end of the harbour lane, and there was the harbour dominated by this massive statue. I just had to get a photograph of 'Verity', so we went out to the end of the harbour wall to find a point where I might be able to fit the whole figure into the viewfinder's frame. Try as I might, it was almost impossible to get a close-up that would bring in the whole statue. I tried every available angle, but it was too difficult. Compromise is often the name of the game in photography, and this happens to be a classic example of that.

It was time for our well-earned meal, so off we went to an atmospheric pub with the date of 1360 on the wall outside. The famous poet, Chaucer, would have been about twenty in that year, long before he wrote *Canterbury Tales*. The meal was most welcome, especially as lunch seemed a distant memory after all the walking we had done since that time.

We slept well that night. The much-talked-of breakfast was better than anticipated, with beautifully fresh bread, real farm butter, and Cheddar cheese with a vintage kick to it. There was also Gorgonzola cheese and my favourite chunky marmalade. Jon's face had that placidity about it that suggested that he too was quite happy with the opulence of this breakfast; it surely could have been much worse. We finished this off with a great-tasting coffee, and we were ready to hit the trail once again… day four and the final day of this phase of our training. Tonight, we could sleep in our own beds.

Jon's phone rang; it was Sue. Her father's health had deteriorated a little more. Jon assured her that he would drive up from Plymouth the following day, unless she wanted him to travel up by train today from Barnstaple. Sue agreed with Jon that he should complete the walk today and drive up early the next day. Jon's four daughters were understandably upset about their grandfather, and Jon was eager to be with them.

Ilfracombe had not started to come to life as we left the town. A steep climb got us back onto the coast path once again, and the sky seemed to promise a great spell of weather for our last day on this section of our walk. It wasn't long before the terrain became more undulating and gentler for a while, but there were a lot more hills waiting for us as the morning progressed.

We reached the big surf beaches of Woolacombe and Croyde by early afternoon. I suggested to Jon that it could be a good idea to hop onto a bus for Barnstaple at Croyde, as this would get us to the rail station by mid-afternoon and back to Plymouth by early evening. Jon agreed that, in view of his early start the following day to travel home to Sue and the girls, this idea worked well for him. The fact that Jon's face turned scarlet with indignation when I once again produced my senior citizen's bus pass to the bus driver was another matter entirely.

Everything went according to plan with our travel arrangements for the return to Plymouth, and I wished Jon well for his long journey up to Reading for the following day. It had been a successful training walk, and we definitely felt the benefit of it. When I consider how close we came to Jon having to cut short the walk from Minehead and return to Reading, we came out of it well.

I thought about the challenges awaiting us on the next phase of the training. That walk, from Barnstaple to Newquay in Cornwall, is particularly demanding. I wondered what characters and incidents we would encounter. One thing was for sure, it wouldn't be dull. Join us again in two weeks' time for the big one!

THIRTEEN

Jon arrived back from Reading in good time to get his gear organised for the Barnstaple to Newquay training walk. His father-in-law was holding his own, but Jon would still have to be on standby in case he received the call to travel home if Ken's condition worsened.

The excitement of getting back onto the coastal footpath was mounting. Looking out of the train windows on the way to Exeter, we saw the countryside sparkling as the sunlight flitted across the morning dew; an archipelago of wispy clouds floating high overhead; rooks and seagulls following a bustling tractor patterning a field with furrows; and a view of the coast at Teignmouth just appearing as the train sped its way down the side of the wide river Tone with its glistening channels of estuary water weaving their way around the mud banks. The nearby sea beckoned the river as it had been doing for vast gulfs of time, and now the sea was beckoning the two of us as well – although we were heading to the north coast of Devon, and this scene was on the south coast – but it would not be long before we would change trains at Exeter to travel on the branch line to Barnstaple and the start of our long walking route to Newquay in Cornwall.

The journey from Exeter to Barnstaple was equally as attractive. Early June had welcomed in fresh foliage and luxuriant green pastures. Lambs leapt joyfully in their apparent spasms of irrepressible energy, while their mothers looked on, sphinx-like, some of them with magpies sitting on their backs searching for ticks and insects in the adult fleeces, a very satisfactory symbiotic relationship, from all accounts.

Barnstaple was the end of the line, and here we were. The weather promised to be kind as we went out of the station to start the walk. The day had been problem-free, so far, but then the first obstacle smacked into us. My rucksack suddenly felt ungainly and uncomfortable. I looked it over and saw that one of the shoulder straps had almost pulled away from its anchor point. It was possible to do a temporary repair, but would it hold for the many rigorous miles and days that lay ahead of us? We agreed that the best plan was to find a sports shop here in Barnstaple and buy a new pack that could be relied on. And that is what we did.

The shop we found didn't have a large range, but I found a rucksack that was strong and well designed, and not only did it have an attractive price on the tag, but it also had a fifteen per cent discount in the current sale. I was more than happy with this replacement, but I could not carry the old one as well throughout the days ahead. The sales assistant offered to dispose of it for me, and I looked down at the pack that was being retired and thought briefly of all the walks on which it had served me well. We went on our merry way, and although the new pack felt a little strange, I knew that I would soon get used to it.

It didn't take us long to pick up the South West Coast Path again as it is just on the edge of Barnstaple. In fact, it is merged with a part of the Tarka Trail which would take us all the way to our first overnight stop in Bideford. But first, let me tell you a little about this Tarka Trail.

It acquired its name from the lovely, but ultimately sad, story of Tarka the Otter, from the pen of Henry Williamson in 1927. The Tarka Trail is a cycling and walking route, ranging over parts of North Devon and Exmoor, and is apparently 180 miles long. This is the longest cycling route in the UK.

The gloomy sky didn't stop the heat from building as we trudged the first few hundred yards along the Tarka Trail. This must be the longest of the rare flat sections on the 630 miles of the whole route from Minehead to Poole in Dorset. Not only was the path flat, but it also threw the heat and humidity back from its several miles of tarmac to torment us. Playful and persistent flies also tormented us, and I made a mental note to buy a trekker's insect net to fit over my bush hat to cover my face and neck when under such an incessant assault.

In spite of this discomfort, there were abundant compensations. The salty tang from the exposed mud flats of the estuary of the River Taw mixed with the smells of the salt marsh stretching out some way from the high water level. The estuary birds clearly loved this environment. There were oyster catchers with their black-and-white plumage and orange beaks, turnstones working along the gravelly beaches and the margins of the mud flats, the usual squadrons of opportunist seagulls, and further out from us, near the edge of the silvery tide, was a curlew with its plaintive, poetic song. There were even two rooks turning over skeins of bladderwrack seaweed to try their luck with any crabs moulting from their shells. The crabs do this in order to enter the soft back stage and then grow a bigger shell to expand into. All of this brought back an opulent treasury of memories about my childhood spent on the estuary beaches of the River Tamar that runs between Plymouth and Cornwall, but if I digress onto that, there will be no telling where our story will take us!

We plodded on, drank plenty of water to counter the effects of the humidity, regularly wiped the sweat from our brows, glanced backwards and forwards to register if we needed to take avoidance measures in view of the increasing numbers of oncoming bicycles, and speculated non-stop about what lay ahead of us over the next five days. I had backpacked some of the route years ago, and I will tell you about one or two of the adventures of that trip when we reach those sections of the walk. But for now, let's press on to

Bideford and, hopefully, a good evening meal and a good night's rest.

As we reached the outskirts of Instow, I noticed that Jon's face had sagged into a haunted, wilted, hungry look. You guessed it – his tapeworm had woken up and was not going to take no for an answer. Then I remembered that we had not eaten anything substantial since breakfast. Normally, at this point, Jon would scrabble inside his pack for one of his favourite 'fillers': a large malt loaf crammed with energy-coursing calories. Alas, he didn't bring one along this time. But all was not lost.

The sun umbrellas of an alfresco tea house, with tempting seafood and other tasty things, loomed up out of a ridge of sand. It was unexpected and even mirage-like to two hungry pilgrims like us. In fact, it was so disorienting that I uncharacteristically offered to buy Jon a lavish mid-afternoon lunch, regardless of the cost, an impulse instantly regretted. Yes, he looked staggered at this gesture and took me up on the offer, not knowing if my attack of generosity would ever be repeated.

My calorie-controlled snack, and Jon's uninhibited, and much more elaborate exploitation of my offer, set us both up well for the final section of the walk to Bideford. We had left the banks of the River Taw, and the walk we had started on now showed the beauty of the River Torridge in its late ebbing, restful state before the incoming tide would push against the river's downflow to cause eddies, currents, and small tide races as it spearheaded its way upriver to Bideford. The sky cast aside its moody cloudscape, and the hazy sunlight enveloped the scene as if it were an impressionistic painting. I could easily imagine the artist Monet sitting in this spot painting his beloved water and the effects of the light mingling with it in a kind of languid duet.

Bideford eventually came into view. It seemed to be bathed in the same silky, late afternoon light, its serenity punctuated by the cries of seagulls as they swooped over the river in search of the fingerling young of mackerel, bass, pollack, and grey mullet, all being swept along by the strengthening incoming tide. Such sensual feasts are, for me, an important part of the lure of the great outdoors. I find it difficult not to be fully mindful of the surroundings and what is happening all around me.

We walked into Bideford feeling that this relatively short walk on the first day of our trip was just right for distance and pace. No hills, no steep cliffs to tackle, no rugged terrain to manoeuvre, but all that would change tomorrow!

The Airbnb was easy to find. Our room had a good view of the river and the main town over the bridge on the other side. The hosts were interesting people to talk with, and they gave us some restaurant recommendations where we could get our evening meal. Breakfast was not part of the deal, so we would need to look around the town that evening to find a place where we could get an early breakfast the next morning.

We settled on Wetherspoon for the meal that evening, and it was so welcoming that we decided that this would be the ideal place for breakfast on the following morning, especially as they opened at 8am. The meal was obliging enough to satisfy Jon's fastidious standards, and my more stoic expectations, and the noticeably discounted drinks all contributed to a pleasant evening.

Eventually, it was time to amble back to the bnb. The heat of the past day had been soothed away by the coolness of the evening, and the peaceful walk back across the bridge, over the placid fish-dimpled river, brought on a pleasant tiredness. Sleep came upon us like exhaustion after a good workout in the gym in our other lives. I let my thoughts drift, and the slowly approaching Kilimanjaro expedition featured prominently until sleep took over.

* * *

Morning opened up another promising day. Even Jon slept soundly that night, and that's unusual for him, so we were raring to go early to get a good breakfast. This third Airbnb was by far the most comfortable one so far on the route from Minehead; third time lucky. We said our goodbyes to the hosts and set out on day two of this second training walk. Our route today would take us via Clovelly to Jon's first experience of Youth Hostels at a place called Elmscott. Only by pushing ourselves very hard indeed would we be able to walk the whole route and to arrive at the hostel in a reasonable time for a meal. The bus service was our saviour. We decided to get the bus in Bideford and get off at a convenient stop for Clovelly. The walk from Clovelly to Elmscott looked all right on the map, but time would tell.

We checked the bus times, and there was enough time for us to get a leisurely breakfast before the journey, so off we went back to Wetherspoon for three-egg omelettes with extras, toast and marmalade, and as much coffee as we could drink after paying for just the first one.

Little did I know at that point that there was a grievous disappointment looming for me and an uplifting, mood-enhancing morning lining up for Jon's enjoyment. This is how it happened. We arrived at the bus stop in good time with about ten minutes to wait. The bus came in, driven by a lady with whom one would think twice before arguing with; she had that look of intractability about her. I stepped onto the bus first and produced my senior citizen's bus pass as usual.

"I'm sorry, but I cannot accept that on this service."

I was floored in the first round. I quickly looked over my shoulder and saw a queue behind Jon waiting to get onto this bus, and it became immediately clear that there was no point in holding up the bus while I tried to find out why I had been denied. Jon's face assumed a simpering, sympathetic look, but he couldn't hide his real pleasure in finally witnessing justice. I had to pay what he had to pay, and it was painful for me, as well as being totally unexpected. As we sat down for the journey, I reflected on how rare real, selfless friendship is in this day and age. I also reflected on why my bus pass, which should be accepted on any scheduled bus service in England, didn't make the grade here in North Devon. It was only when we got off the bus near Clovelly that I was able to ask the lady driver why bus passes were not accepted in this area.

"You showed your pass at 9.27am, and the free service doesn't start until 9.30am in this area."

Jon burst out laughing, and after a few fuming moments, I laughed with him. Even the lady driver allowed a self-satisfied smirk to dimple her obdurate cheeks. The laugh was well and truly on me that morning.

* * *

We walked down the steep, cobbled lane through this remarkable village of Clovelly. I was surprised to learn that the whole village had apparently been given to his wife by William the Conqueror back in the eleventh century, and it is still privately owned.

The Red Lion pub at the very bottom of the cobbled lane is part of the small harbour setting, and we decided to sit outside the pub and have a quiet cup of coffee before setting off on our walk again. I knew from previous experience what lay ahead of us, and a rest at this stage seemed like a good idea.

You remember Richard Jackelman who was with our walking group on the St Ives to Lamorna training walk back in that muddy April. Well, he was performing here on one occasion with his sea shanty singing group – 'The Old Gaffers' – when a strange thing happened.

It was on a Sunday afternoon in spring, and there was a chilly wind blowing in from the east. After singing two or three shanties outdoors on the harbour wall, the group decided to head for the bar in the Red Lion and, if anyone asked them, they would sing another couple of shanties to show willing.

The bar was very quiet when the shanty group went in, but the large audience listening to them out on the harbour wall followed them into the bar. The singing group was coaxed into singing some more shanties, and after a few minutes of hectic custom, the barman told the group that it was too noisy for him to serve his customers. The group, not wishing to cause any trouble, moved out of the bar and back onto the harbour wall. It must have been a shock to the barman to see not just the singing group leave the bar but virtually all his customers as well, as they just couldn't get enough sea shanties to satisfy them. Perhaps the story of the Pied Piper Shanty Group of Clovelly will be passed down as part of the folklore of the village!

We finished our coffees, had a final look out over the harbour, and set off on the steep, steep climb back up through the amazing village to rejoin the coastal footpath.

As we plodded up the sloping cobbles, I reminded us both that this was a valuable training opportunity for Kilimanjaro in three months' time. I even wondered if Kilimanjaro would be as steep as Clovelly Village; that thought came back to ridicule me as we later pushed ourselves hard up the mountain at a very slow pace in a punishing, oxygen-depleted, much steeper environment. But that's a story for another day.

We eventually reached the top of the village and found the continuation of the coastal footpath. The weather had changed from being fairly bright to being a little more morose, but the rain that seemed to be threatening us did not materialise. Our next port of call would be Hartland Point, but hill after hill after hill awaited us before we reached it. Our legs were telling us that this way of training was really paying off.

* * *

We shortly found ourselves in another of the rare, wooded areas of the coastal path between Minehead and Penzance. It was certainly a contrast to the largely open seascapes and landscapes we had encountered so far on this trip, and we enjoyed the birdsong and being bathed in fir tree fragrances. The only problem I had with this part of the walk sprang from my memory of my first trek through these woods many years ago and how the glum weather then was being replicated now. The weather then was merely a prelude to what happened during the rest of that day and into the following day when my walking companion and I reached Hartland Point. But let's leave that story until a little later.

We emerged from the woodland and into the start of our hill-climbing sequence. This was good training ground for us, and the rugged coastline fed us with view after view of awesome rocky cliffs as they loomed over the vicious-looking reefs running out to sea. Wrecking was quite an industry in this part of the world. By showing false signals from lanterns used in adverse weather situations, ships could sometimes be lured onto rocks or onto beaches from which there would be no escape, either for the ships or for their doomed crews who wouldn't have been allowed to report what had befallen them to the authorities. Desperate poverty and ruthless greed were so prevalent in those times that wrecking served both motivations. Imagine a sailor, having survived his ship being wrecked, struggling ashore and then being clubbed to death by the perpetrators during the course of their looting of the ship's cargo as it was washed ashore, along with survivors, in a critical state.

We eventually reached the last part of the trek leading to Hartland Point. A man stood on the coast path just in front of us, and he was clearly looking intently for something way down in the cove far below us. Jon started a conversation with him, and we soon started to get local information about the wildlife in the vicinity. He pointed out some seal activity in the sea below us and lent us his binoculars to get a better view of what was happening. This gentleman had also spotted dolphins in the cove on various occasions and even a peregrine falcon. It really is inspiring to talk with such keen observers of the natural world, and he inspired us to be even more watchful as we continued this walk of ours.

Hartland Point glowered under the morose sky. Memories came flooding back to me about that backpacking trip along this section of coast many years ago. The sky on that occasion wasn't just morose, it was menacing. On this occasion, I was backpacking with a friend called Ian, a civil engineer and keen walker. We had travelled up to Bideford by coach on a Friday afternoon, and the intention was to walk to Bude in Cornwall, a distance of about forty-five miles, and be collected by Ian's wife on the Sunday evening to drive us back to Plymouth. I told Jon our story in outline, but here is the fuller version of what happened to us and the lessons we learned about backpacking, lessons that have stayed with me ever since.

* * *

Ian had telephoned me during the previous few days to ask me if I was interested in going on this walk. I told him about my backpacking trip on the previous weekend on the coastal footpath between St Ives and Penzance. The weather had been wonderful for the first weekend in April, and I was certainly up for another walk this weekend as the weather had continued to be warm and pleasant. Wild camping was the plan, and we would need a two-man tent. Ian's tent was too heavy for backpacking, and although I had a good-quality one-man tent, my old two-man was relatively cheap and of untested quality in adverse weather conditions. In any event, the weather promised to be kind to us so the tent should have been adequate for this weekend.

Our coach arrived in Bideford in brilliant sunshine to seemingly confirm our good judgement about taking on this trip in early April. We set off through the town, zipping past Appledore, increasing the pace even more until we arrived at Westward Ho!, still congratulating ourselves on our good luck in choosing this weekend for the trip, when the sky darkened. The wind increased. The sand whipped off the beach and stung us with its force. Westward Ho! took on a sinister appearance, and we were presented with a premonition of what this place might be like on a bleak winter's day. Having a home on the Atlantic-facing coast may seem like living the dream, but be careful what you wish for!

We pressed on, soon reaching the edge of Westward Ho!, and we barely saw anyone else out walking. The true coastal footpath opened up ahead of us, and the weather seemed to become a little more friendly. After covering a good distance, and with the evening beginning to close in, we started to look for our first night's campsite.

The only relatively flat ground we came across was over a wire fence and a low hedge and on the top edge of a reasonably flat, grassy bank that rolled away down into a valley. This would certainly do for a campsite, so up went the tent. We had plenty of water with us to prepare the meal, and while I started to prepare it, Ian brewed the welcome mugs of tea.

Although I lay claim to the credit for it myself, the meal was pretty good. The first course was a thick soup with chunks of fresh Bideford bread. Textured vegetable protein with a tasty stock, augmented with rehydrated powdered potato and rehydrated peas, formed the nourishing main course. Dessert came in the form of rehydrated stewed apple, made memorable by thin, pourable custard. All of this was managed by a careful sequencing of bringing one part of the main meal to a bubbling heat, removing it to simmer for a while, during which time the veg was put onto the stove to rehydrate. The main part of the meal was then reheated to complete the preparations. The principle behind this type of food was to provide high-energy food with low bulk for carrying. As long as water was available at, or somewhere close to, the campsite, the weight of food could be minimised for much of the time.

Coffee, sitting around the stove, together with campfire yarns, took us pleasantly into the early, but sinister, sunset. The evening chill signalled that it was time to turn in and get rested in preparation for what the next day would bring. Campers often find that the first night out can be less than comfortable, but we coped with it quite well that night.

We awoke just after dawn, and it was surprisingly cold. I opened the tent door flaps, and there was a crinkly sound. Yes, there had been a heavy frost overnight, and the tent had a thin coating of ice that sparkled in the first beams of sunlight like an array of sequins.

Ian prepared the scrambled eggs and bacon, toast, and coffee, while I sorted out the tent and gear for the day ahead. We decided to let the sun thaw out the tent before we tried to pack it away. Just as we were enjoying our coffee, a huge dog fox slunk within a few yards of us. I threw some buttered crusts in his direction, and he tucked into these with relish before moving silently, and enigmatically, away again into the cover of the hedgerows. Quite a sight!

We set off on the trail again before 8am. The path dropped down close to the sea, and the morning promised a settled day ahead. To our surprise, there was an old wreck of a freighter listed right over on the unforgiving rocks. What an awful thing it must be to experience such an event, the ship you are on being at the mercy of the savage waves as they drive the vessel relentlessly towards the vicious endgame! In retrospect, this could have been seen as an omen of what was waiting in store for us later that day. But in the meantime, we walked on in gentle sunshine, looking forward to reaching Clovelly in time for a pint of beer. Neither of us had visited Clovelly before, but its reputation as being an atmospheric old Devon fishing village was legendary.

Moody clouds had gathered by the time we reached the village. The steepness of the cobbled lane running down through the village deserved its reputation, and I felt sorry for the early holidaymakers who were struggling over the rough surface in flimsy shoes and even flip-flops. I had heard that donkeys had been used in the village for many years to haul fish and exhausted visitors back up to the top of the long and mountain-steep lane. We didn't see any donkeys, but a battered Land Rover was providing an identical service that afternoon.

The Red Lion pub at the bottom of the hill on the harbour wall looked inviting. While we were enjoying a glass of ale, the need to press on if we were to keep to a reasonable schedule entered the conversation, and it was decided to aim for Hartland Point for our overnight camp. This would put us in a good position to reach our destination at Bude in reasonable time on Sunday. Ian's wife would be able to collect us from Bude and get us back to Plymouth by early Sunday evening, in good time to get everything ready for the working week.

The weather outside the pub was turning sour: scudding clouds coming in fast from the north, a finger-numbing wind blowing straight in from the malignant grey sea, one or two of the local fishermen looking at the sky and shaking their heads – even the seagulls were retreating inland. But perhaps the main sign that things were worrying was the general exodus from the pub as the locals headed home at a rate of knots from their traditional Saturday lunchtime relaxation.

We dug deep and sped back up the cobbled hill. Back on the coastal footpath, we soon entered a wood. As darkening and ominous as it was in the open, here in the woodland it was forbidding, even menacing.

The terrain from the edge of the wood to Hartland Point was over seven miles of quite tricky walking. Rain started to intimidate us on and off, but it was the increasing strength of the wind that had us worried. We needed to find a sheltered spot to set up camp at or near Hartland Point, but the map didn't look too encouraging given the northerly direction of the increasing wind.

Hartland Point eventually came into view. It looked dismal, uninviting, and clearly wide open to the elements in their worsening mood. But time was passing, and we needed to pitch camp and get a meal under way before the heavens opened with a vengeance.

We found what seemed to be our best hope of a campsite about a mile down the coast from Hartland Point. It didn't face directly into the wind, which was now approaching gale force, and it did have a stream nearby and a relatively flat grassy area. It would have been an ideal camping spot had the weather been on our side.

Up went the tent in double quick time, and we both walked over to the stream about fifty yards away to fetch water for the meal and to clean up the billycans from breakfast time. I looked back in the direction of the tent when we had almost finished these tasks, but it had disappeared.

The tent had been flattened. The two aluminium poles had been bent and twisted into mocking 'v' shapes by the wind, and they were beyond repair. At this point, the rain lashed into us with the venom of an angered weather god taking it out on us personally. We knew that this weather was going to get worse, but its severity was beginning to feel dangerous, even life-threatening.

By putting the backpacks back-to-back inside the flattened tent, we were able to get a little elevation from the violently flapping nylon material of the tent and its groundsheet. We secured the tent pegs as much as we could into the stony ground. It was obvious by this time that cooking the evening meal couldn't even be considered. We checked our food supplies for anything viable to keep us going and came up with two small chocolate bars, a little cereal with fruit in it, an oxo cube, a little bread past its best, and, joy of joys, a miniature bottle containing a double measure of brandy from the first aid kit reserved for emergencies, and our present predicament qualified as a real emergency, as far as we were concerned. Supper, as you can imagine, was a frugal affair. Not only that, but we were quite wet from the bad weather. There should have been another hour or so of daylight, but the light outside the tent was almost gone. We changed into our dry clothing with difficulty because of the lack of elevation in the shaking tent, but at least the slack tent material was keeping us safe from the merciless wind and pelting rain outside.

Sleep that night was elusive. The shaking tent and groundsheet made a terrific racket, and I had just dropped off to sleep on several occasions when the noise of the wind-tormented tent shook so violently that we thought it was going to rip wide open. What a nightmare that would have been!

I woke up first the following morning, and the wind had moderated to some extent. My clothes were saturated. Then I remembered that, during the cold night, we had decided to get inside our large polythene survival bags. I had never had to use one of these things before and didn't realise that although the bag would protect you from the worst of the weather, the accumulating condensation from body heat gradually made everything inside the bag soggy, which is what happened to me. Ian woke up and had the same problem. So now we had two wet sets of clothing and nothing else to change into. But I was about to find out about another problem just outside the ravaged tent.

Looking out of the almost horizontal tent doorway, I saw that the surrounding coast and countryside had a covering of snow. Not only that, but it was snowing quite heavily as I looked out over the scene, and it was bitterly cold, but there's more. The wind, which had moderated, was now increasing and driving the snow along in such spasms that it was obscuring the landscape. Was this turning into a blizzard? Ian found it difficult to believe me when I relayed all this to him, but a quick look outside made him groan with horror at the spectacle.

Breakfast, just like the previous evening's meal, was out of the question. Perhaps it was just as well that we didn't drink the brandy last night, because now it could be a lifesaver. That was the first time that I had breakfasted on brandy, and I haven't been able to bring myself to drink it since that deeply memorable morning.

There was no viable escape route that we knew of, so we decided to press on towards Morwenstow with our fingers crossed that the weather would let us get there. The map showed that there was a pub in the village, and who knows, it could even have a log fire and perhaps the chance to buy a good meal.

With the gear packed and the backpacks heavy with moisture, we set off up the steep climb to the clifftop, and what cliffs we saw that morning. They were high enough to make even eagles feel queasy, and the coast path was close to the edge of vast drop-offs to the rock-strewn coastline below us. Not only that, but the wind had shifted to blow offshore, driving the large snowflakes along towards the sea in huge flurries that almost blanketed out our visibility. The fact that the wind seemed to find huge satisfaction in pushing against our backpacks, and almost levering us off the edges of the cliffs, was an added and frightening feature in this land of elemental savagery. I reminded myself about the idyllic side of nature the previous weekend while walking between St Ives and Penzance and made an unshakeable decision that this present experience would not put me off backpacking. My admiration and deep respect for the vagaries of nature had leapfrogged over all this, and it gave me the strength to continue dragging my sodden and heavy clothing and gear up and down whatever presented itself in front of us, regardless of the hunger that was now pleading to be assuaged.

Something else clamoured in my mind for attention, and that was the overdue need to invest in the best gear and backpacking clothing that I could afford. This day sealed that commitment into my mind like rapid-hardening cement gripping onto a structure of steel girders designed to last a lifetime. I also knew now the importance of packing the type of gear that could engage with blizzards, if necessary, and still come out fighting at the end of it. When fellow walkers sometimes say to me that I seem to be carrying a lot of gear in my backpack, I try to paint them a picture of nature's tempestuous traps waiting for the unwary, perhaps to kill them. Whether this message gets through to them is difficult to say, but at least I make an effort to share the lessons learned during this Homeric trip.

Ian and I were feeling the worse for wear as we eventually approached the steep climb up to Morwenstow. We were weakening, cold wrenched at our willpower, breathing wheezed away like geriatric steam engines, snow swirled tauntingly and seeped into our clothing, snow-covered rocks tried to trip us, but all of this faded away as the village with its pub came into view.

The pub was surprisingly busy. A log fire flared out its welcome into the jolly bar area with goodwill to all comers on this difficult day. Ian and I, like heat-seeking vagabonds, soaked up this thermal nectar and smiled with relief. The locals in the bar could see how far gone we were and showed their concern. Some kind lady and gentleman brought us over a large glass of mulled wine each, and that really hit the spot. In fact, on empty stomachs, the hot and fragrant wine slammed into us like a playful wrecking ball. All of this seemed to endear us to the customers in the pub. There weren't any meals being served, but the landlord's wife brought us some cheese sandwiches and refused to take any payment for them. As the steam curled up from our wet clothing, and little pools of water formed all around on the flagstones where we were standing, we started to think about our way ahead on this day of suffering and kindness.

People asked us where we were hoping to get to when we left the village. We told them about our plan to reach Bude and meet up with Ian's wife who would drive us back to Plymouth. One gentleman apologetically explained that the snow had made it impossible to get through on the linking roads to virtually all parts of the county; we were marooned on the north (Devon) coast. Not only that, but we were emphatically advised not to attempt to get to Bude while this weather persisted. The landlord ushered Ian over to the bar and handed him the telephone to ring his wife to explain our predicament. She was relieved to hear from us and said that she would telephone my mother to bring her up to date on everything.

At this point, two local angels came to our rescue. They were a husband-and-wife team who had recently moved to Morwenstow from the Midlands. They had bought a guest house just outside the village and were almost at the end of renovation work before opening up to visitors for the coming season. The offer to stay with them until we could travel back to Plymouth was accepted without hesitation and with great relief, even joy. And so it was that we were taken in like orphans from the blizzard.

The guest house had age and great atmosphere. Another log fire radiated out its warm welcome as we entered the living room, and Margaret and Eric started to work out the best way to start drying our clothing and gear. We were escorted to our respective rooms, and each bedroom had an en suite with a huge and luxurious bath. Margaret planned to have a meal ready for us in about an hour and a half, so there was plenty of time to take a leisurely bath and get settled in.

I remember that meal to this day, about forty years later. It was a magnificent Sunday roast after a warming oxtail soup, and a raspberry meringue with Cornish clotted cream completed the heavenly meal, the first substantial meal since breakfast early on the previous day. The excellent and fragrant wine flowed while we all talked away in front of the log fire. At one point, I started to wonder how much all of this wonderful hospitality would cost us. I always carry enough money with me to cover most unexpected expenses, but this was something else, and I had no idea how much Ian had brought with him. But the warmth of our welcome, and the heady wine, helped me to put that to the back of my mind until the time of reckoning.

Sleep rippled over me that night like gentle wavelets embracing a warm, sandy beach. The tiredness and effort of the past twenty-four hours finally drew me into a deep vortex of sleep where even dreams dared not to intrude.

A strange light enveloped me as I woke up several hours later. It was strong sunlight that poured in through the bedroom window on a beautiful spring day in this unforgettable month of April. Eric brought me in a cup of tea and gave me the news that it had just been confirmed on the radio that the roads across our part of Devon were open again, thanks to the efforts of the snow plough teams who had worked through the night. The road to Plymouth had been opened up along the whole route, and we could start working on a plan to get back to our homes.

Margaret had prepared a magnificent breakfast for everyone, and even Gilbert the Labrador dragged himself out of his comfortable basket near the Aga cooking and heating range to try his luck for the odd sausage or two that might be looking for any takers.

It was another big surprise when Eric said that he and Margaret had been planning a shopping trip to Plymouth for the past two or three weeks, and with the lovely weather outside, this seemed like too good a chance to miss. In addition to this, they would be delighted to help us get back to rejoin our families. Their generosity was overwhelming. Not only that, but when we settled the bill, it was way under what we expected. We tried to persuade them to take a more realistic sum, but they wouldn't hear of it. By helping us in our time of need, they explained that it also helped them by doing a trial run for the guests who had already started to book with them.

We arrived back safely in Plymouth and took our leave of these two lovely people. I stayed with them again a year or two later, and they were doing deservedly well with their new business. I often think of them both and their great kindness when we were very much in need of friends. This whole experience inspired me to always offer help to anyone in a difficult situation, especially fellow backpackers.

* * *

Jon listened to this dramatic backpacking story as we covered another five or so miles along the coast path. Before long, we turned inland up a steep-sided valley on our way to Jon's first experience of staying in a hostel, run in this instance by the Youth Hostel Association. Getting to the Elmscott Hostel meant climbing a long and steep hill, and after a full day's hiking on the coast path, this felt unjust, but then we remembered what we were training for and recalled from the experiences of previous climbers that Kilimanjaro would be unrelenting in the challenges it was preparing for us when we attempted to climb it in three months' time.

Elmscott Hostel crowned the top of the hill in all its unrelenting dowdiness, and I wondered what Jon would make of it when we went inside. I had stayed in three or four quite pleasant hostels belonging to the YHA over the years, but Elmscott was much more spartan. Jon's face and posture folded into unaccustomed defeat as he looked around the place. The dormitory was rather cramped and dated, but the double rooms were a little better. The husband and wife who were running the hostel on a volunteer basis for a week or two invited us to stay in the pick of the rooms as there weren't any other bookings that night. Jon's mood rose a little but only just perceptibly. Should I remind him yet again that we should only expect basic accommodation in some of the hostels, or would that be inflammatory? But even with this introduction to hostel life, I think he would still prefer this to wild camping. I would have been overjoyed to find such a refuge on the day of the blizzard.

We knew from the write-up about the hostel that there was a small shop on the premises, so we only had basic provisions with us. There were tins of soup, tins of vegetables, tinned pasta dishes, and even tins of fruit. Milk and eggs were available and so were potatoes, sachets of coffee, and tea bags. Jon thought that the prices were steep, but we had to bear in mind that someone had to bring these items in from quite some distance away, and it was convenient to have food here rather than have to carry it uphill and down dale from Clovelly. In the event, the cost of the meal worked out very reasonably indeed, and Jon made a good job of cooking it in the communal kitchen. I fiendishly pointed out to Jon during our dessert that we only had another six overnight stays in hostels during the remainder of our training walks. He became so indignant that he almost choked on a slice of tinned pineapple. It was clear to me then that weaning himself away from fine wining and dining in quality hotels could present him with one of the most memorable challenges of his life, but I knew that he would do it for the sake of our training. A saving grace was that there would be the odd occasion when he could indulge his finer tastes. I was thinking of the fish restaurants in coastal towns like Port Isaac and St Ives and maybe in Bude the following evening.

I slept well that night, and according to Jon, I didn't snore, a real bonus as far as he was concerned. Jon prepared a good breakfast for us to set us up for (according to the map) a strenuous day of hill training ahead. We said our goodbyes to the pleasant and helpful couple who were looking after the hostel and stepped out into a lovely day.

There was a convenient path close by the hostel, and this led straight out over the fields to the coastal footpath. Wildflowers were abundant, and lambs frolicked among them on this memorable June morning. It didn't take long to reach the coast with its smooth sea and clear blue sky right out to the horizon.

This idyll only lasted for the short walk before we started hitting the hill climbs: steep, precarious, geared to walkers out to punish themselves, chivvied along by the squawks of sneering seagulls, sweating freely, and, in a way, thoroughly getting into the spirit of it all.

We had temporarily lost track of the geography of this day's walk, so when we stumbled across the border marker between Devon and Cornwall later in the morning, it was fitting to congratulate ourselves in having walked so far:

Crossing the border from Devon into Cornwall

Minehead, our starting point back up the coast in Somerset, seemed like a long way away, and Devon had presented us with many steep cliffs and hills for our training. Now that we were just about to start the big walks in Cornwall, the excitement started to build even more than all the previous days that we had walked and climbed this long, long trail. The landscape had changed considerably during our time on this coastal path, but the seascapes had remained our constant inspirations to walk onwards to see what the coast had in store for us around the next headland and then the next:

An unexpected encounter on the coastal footpath: two friendly goats smell the cheddar cheese in my pack

*Two more goats appeared a little later, but
these were apparently wild, with much bigger horns!*

We strode out into the west, its headlands shimmering in the haze of the morning sun, the sea a turquoise mirror, a wonder of nature, the gulls sailing with effortless grace on the clifftop thermals and with a breeze just gentle enough to keep us cool on the hill climbs as we plodded on towards Morwenstow. Yes! The same Morwenstow Ian and I just managed to reach on the day of the blizzard all those years ago.

Morwenstow came into view, and it was totally different from the way it appeared as it came into our view on that fateful, and yet so memorable, day of the frightful blizzard. Today, the village was overbrimming with delightful flowers in gardens and hedgerows, and the amazing fragrances attracted bees in their nectared ecstasy. Beautiful old stone buildings with their lichened garden walls and fragrant rose gardens seemed like a dream from a previous age. The old church sat like an ancient sage bestowing blessings on all who walked by. One could imagine its famous vicar in times past, the Reverend Hawker, looking out from his study window upon this small, but rather wonderful, old village. He was well known in his day for his deep concern for shipwrecked mariners along this notoriously wild and dangerous coastline. He built a hut on the sea cliffs, from what appears to be timber from wrecked ships, and sat in the hut for hours at a time, sometimes composing hymns and sermons, at other times looking out over the sea to still his mind, and, in bad weather, to watch out for any ships that might be in trouble. This tiny hut had become famous over the years, and it is now in the care of the National Trust and open to the public.

The pub where Ian and I had found refuge and wonderful friends on the day of the blizzard was not open at that time in the morning, but we found a delightful tea garden instead. The garden was an oasis of calm, even in the tranquillity of the village, with bees humming around the flowers, small birds flitting and chirruping all around the garden, the tinkle of water somewhere close by, and cheeky sparrows landing on our wooden table full of expectancy that we would share some of the tea garden's excellent cakes with them. The tea from the lustrous chinaware was so welcome that we had three cups each.

Before we left, I found an opportunity to ask if the Good Samaritans who took Ian and me into their care on the day of the blizzard were still living in the guest house just outside the village. It seems that they retired several years ago and moved away, probably to be nearer their family. I will never forget them and their kindness. I have thought about them from time to time throughout my life since then and have tried to live by their kind example. If by any chance Eric and Margaret should ever read this book, I send them heartfelt greetings and my thanks for being so inspirational to me. We had to drag ourselves away from the tea garden, an oasis also of excellent tea and cakes, enhanced by calm and shade on this sun-filled day that was warming up considerably.

Bude was quite a distance away, and the heat persuaded us to walk along the country lanes for a few miles before rejoining the coastal footpath at Coombe Valley. This would save some time and give us a better chance to reach Bude in reasonably comfortable time to find our Airbnb, have a cooling shower, and hit the town for a nice meal and a long, cool drink.

By the time we reached Coombe Valley, the heat had increased even more. A busy, and unexpected, cafe came into view as we walked down into the valley, and the thought of a cold drink and an ice cream overpowered any resistance we might have had. A beautiful afternoon, the soothing sound of small waves rolling up the nearby beach, the cooling and fragrant influence of an icy-cold elderflower drink, the call of two buzzards high up overhead, the wispy clouds drifting lazily across the great blue dome of the sky; how were we going to drag ourselves away from this foretaste of paradise on the Cornish coast?

We eventually found the resolve to hoist the backpacks onto our shoulders again and head for the steep cliffs taunting us on the far side of the valley. Once we were under way again, the scenery became softer in some respects. At one point, we came across a big spread of wild irises or flag as they are also called. Some lambs frolicked near the irises, and the scene was captivating. Yet something else took our attention. The scene opening up for us just ahead was a really attractive and long, sandy beach. The map showed that this was close to Bude, our destination for today.

Bude soon came into view in all its sun-drenched glory. I had only visited Bude twice before and that was many years ago, and on both days, the weather had been cold, grey, threatening, and off-putting; the kind of day when it is a real pleasure to get back to the coach park and head for home. But today was something else entirely. Surfers were out in large numbers, even though the legendary Bude waves had taken a siesta. But like they say, 'you don't always need the big waves to have a great day's surfing'. The perfect wave could be somewhere out in the Atlantic Ocean heading for Bude with increasing attitude; maybe it will hit the beach tomorrow.

We found our Airbnb quite easily, and it was within the sound of the lapping waves and the ozone-laden salt tang from the beach. What we didn't know was that we were staying in the home of a UK surfing champion. The young man's welcoming family ran the accommodation, and he was living the dream. I think we both wished secretly that we could have stayed for a few days and taken surfing lessons from this impressive young man.

Our accommodation happened to be in a nicely converted, large, wooden garden outhouse. It had everything we needed to make us comfortable, and I tried to imagine what surfing guests the place had sheltered in the course of its history as a bed and breakfast haven; the mind boggles!

We found a pleasant restaurant for our evening meal near the surf beach, over which the sun was beginning to reach out lazily for the horizon. It was great just to relax after three days of hard training in hot weather, and we talked about the many things we had seen since setting out from Barnstaple. The time passed pleasantly until it was time to get some rest in preparation for whatever the next day would bring, so back we went to the 'surf shack' for a final mug of coffee before turning in for the night.

FOURTEEN

The new day brought a sky-coloured mood of multi-shaded grey, and the sea almost mirrored this in its silvery way. It was a symphony in silver and grey but with a restrained beauty that permeated the senses. But where had the blue sky, hot sun, June mellowness, and the tropical feel of yesterday gone? It had evaporated. Yet, even at 8am, surfers were paddling out over the lively waves, their boards shooting back like surf-scattering arrows towards the beach as soon as a promising wave lifted them up and hurled them into a fast and impressive slither.

Jon had prepared our breakfast back at the surf shack, and we felt ready for the day, whatever it had in store for us. We had enjoyed our stay in the atmospheric accommodation, and we had also very much enjoyed the evening in the town.

Our destination today was Boscastle, about sixteen miles away over rough and testing terrain. The map indicated that this would be a demanding training route that could take us several hours. The intended accommodation for the night ahead was to be in the Youth Hostel in Boscastle. I had stayed there once before when trekking along this section of coast, but that was many years past. The hostel has been completely refurbished since that time after a shocking event, but more of that story when we get there.

We felt sad as we said farewell to Bude, and the plaintive cry of the gulls echoed our feelings. What is it about seagulls? Most people I talk to about these spectacular birds seem to be either indifferent to them or would like to see them culled to the point of extinction. To me – having spent my childhood years in a seagull-rich environment, listening to them as I played on our estuary beaches, pausing while digging in the mud for fishing bait to watch them swirl and glide in the thermals over the wide River Tamar, standing in awe as bass and mackerel drove the small fry up from the depths of the river to feast on them when they had been concentrated, only to see many of these small fry fall victim to the various types of gull marauding from above, and finally, at the end of each day, listening to them as they settled down for the night up in the chimney stacks of the nearby riverside cottages – seashore and harbour towns would be the poorer for their absence. But keep your fish and chips, pasties and even ice creams under proper protection; these coastal tourist town gulls are audacious bandits.

We had to walk a route that ran in close parallel to the busy coast road for eight or nine miles. But we shouldn't complain; the path all the way from where we started, in far-away Minehead, had very few close encounters with roads in the whole of the 124 miles we had walked so far.

At a point about four or five miles along the coast path from Bude, we reached another surfing beach at Widemouth Bay. Its significance to us was important for a striking reason. According to the South West Coast Path Association's annotated map, by walking up and down the great cliffs and hills from Minehead to this point on the coast path, we had achieved the same height gain and loss as if we had walked from sea level to the top of Mount Everest and all the way down to sea level again. What about that for part of our training programme to climb Mount Kilimanjaro!

This put an extra spring in our steps as we gradually made our way to the lunch stop in Crackington Haven. We found a pleasant cafe and had lunch by a picture window with a view of the sea. This also gave us a great view of something we could do without: thick drizzle rolling in from seawards. Luckily, it had passed over by the time we set off on the trail again, but we had our waterproofs at the ready just in case.

The seascapes were striking, and some of the names of the rock promontories were just as striking. I was particularly taken with the name of a small sandy beach called The Strangles, quite alluring. The name may have referred to thick fronds of kelp on the rocks nearby, just waiting to coil, python-like, around the bodies of unfortunate swimmers if they swam close enough to the reefs when the kelp was submerged by a lively high tide.

There were several atmospheric coves along this stretch of coast, and the coast path made us work our leg muscles hard. Seabirds of various types haunted the cliffs and coves, with the occasional 'cronk' of a raven thrown into the mix of raucous maritime melodies.

Boscastle loomed up from behind a headland, and what a striking sight it was with its long and narrow harbour. There were a few boats bobbing, a light drizzle moistening everything, children crabbing on the harbour wall, the steep-sided walls of the valley dreaming in the drizzle, cottages leaning over with age, and visitors ambling around with the look of deeply disoriented fish out of water.

The Youth Hostel was the first building we came to. It would not be open for another hour, so we found a promising pub and attended to our serious dehydration problems. The customers appeared to be a mixture of locals and visitors, and the pub was welcoming. We studied the menu and decided that this place would suit us for our meal, so a table was booked for that evening.

The drizzle outside had increased to rain, so we decided to get into the hostel, get sorted out, and make some coffee. As hostels go, this one in Boscastle is good. The smells of the sea, boats, and fish were right on the doorstep; what more could we ask for?

With everything sorted out, we made our way to the lounge. The kitchen was alongside the lounge, so making coffee didn't present us with a problem. Then, after a brief discussion about the day's walk, we started looking at the hostel's collection of national media coverage of Boscastle's massive deluge of flood water that smashed into the village in 2004. There were also many written accounts about the disaster from residents of the village. It must have been a tremendous ordeal for everyone who was involved in saving their own lives, the lives of other people, and setting about the clean-up when it became safe to move about the village again. If you have access to YouTube on the internet, just enter Boscastle flooding, and be prepared to see some horrendous sights. Sights like large campervans being pushed along furiously towards the harbour by the deep torrent of water ripping through the village and even demolishing buildings.

Perhaps the most telling thing from our point of view was a photograph taken inside the hostel of the room we were now sitting in. The flood water had risen right up to the ceiling as the water just flooded through the whole building from end to end like water gushing through a giant conduit.

The hostel has been nicely refurbished and looks totally different from the first time I stayed there about forty years ago. On that occasion, I met an American cyclist called Brett. He ran a flourishing business escorting American cyclists on some of Britain's interesting cycle routes and was then in Cornwall seeking out new routes for his future groups. I think the numerous big hills might have been a drawback in those days with only basic gearing on bikes.

Brett told me about the wide range of people who came on his trips from America. But what really stuck in my mind was the story of two or three very wealthy customers who were happy struggling along with their cycling groups but whose wives followed along behind the groups in expensive hire cars, usually driven by chauffeurs, and on one occasion, the car was a top-of-the-range Rolls Royce driven by an immaculately turned-out driver in a stunning uniform. Brett confided in me that the tips he received at the end of such tours were supremely generous; nice work if you can get it!

The meal back at the pub that evening was excellent, the atmosphere congenial, and the noise level low enough for us to easily discuss our plan for the following day's walk. This route coming up tomorrow was always going to be the trickiest one of the whole of the three separate training sessions taking us from Minehead to Penzance, and the reason for that was partly the amount of ground we had to cover to get us to our next overnight stop at Treyarnon Bay and partly because of the need to cross the River Camel by ferry from Rock to Padstow. I had tried unsuccessfully to contact the ferry operators in an effort to find out the ferry times for this early part of the year before the main holiday season started. I was also anxious to find out the time of the last ferry of the day so that we could plan our walk in the certainty that we wouldn't be stranded on the beach overnight at Rock.

We had booked several weeks ago to stay the night at the Treyarnon Bay Youth Hostel, and we had also booked and paid for our evening meal and breakfast in advance. The hostel had a good reputation and was in a great location, almost right on the surfing beach. I was sure that Jon would find this hostel more to his liking. Our plan for the following day had to get us to Treyarnon by early evening in time for that meal. With an outline plan in mind, we came to the conclusion that we had no chance of reaching our destination if we didn't use public transport some of the time. With that in mind, we checked out the bus times from Boscastle to as close to Trebarwith Strand as possible for the following morning, and this could give us just the leverage we needed to get us to Rock before the ferry stopped for the day.

There was a bus at about 8.30am, but it had a real problem for me. It was an hour too early for me to use my senior citizen's bus pass; I would have to join Jon and pay for the journey. Jon made a big thing of sympathising with me, but his mocking tone of voice said it all. In any event, we needed to use the bus to stay on schedule.

The hostel dormitory had at least two snorers in it with their volume turned up to full power, and it seems that I was one of them. How Jon manages to carry on with such fitful sleep in such an environment, I will never know. Perhaps he is really asleep and merely dreams that people are snoring and keeping him awake!

Yet again, Jon zipped into the new day and prepared breakfast down in the kitchen while I shaved. Jon has a rather fine beard and doesn't need to shave so is always ahead of me in the mornings.

We took our leave of Boscastle with a certain regret; it really does have something unique about it. Our bus was on time. Being an optimist, I produced my bus pass, and, for whatever reason, it was accepted. I was astonished, and Jon was as indignant as a holidaymaker having his pasty snatched from his hand by an exultant and shameless seagull. Later in our travels, I discovered that not all areas use the same official times for accepting bus passes, and that probably explains it. A pity that, and I thought it was my natural charm that saved me a few pounds on that bus journey!

The bus dropped us at the top of a long country lane leading down to Trebarwith Strand. We passed by several attractive cottages on the way down to the coast, and the valley setting echoed to the birdsong all around us.

Trebarwith Strand itself gave a very real sense of the Atlantic Ocean on the doorstep. It is a surfing beach, as well as being a good beach in its own right. We stayed for a while to take in the exhilarating view of the alluring sea and Gull Island and to watch a collie dog trying to hold a conversation with a large pebble that was draped in green silkweed. But time was of the essence today, so off we set on the demanding coastal path towards Port Isaac, a journey of about six hilly miles.

Port Isaac has become famous over the past few years. The popular *Doc Martin* television series was filmed almost exclusively in the village and the immediate area. The village was renamed Port Wen for the purpose of the film's story, but I don't think the locals minded too much in view of the revenue the filming brought to the village. Another well-received film was also recently filmed here, and that was *Fisherman's Friends*.

We reached the top of the hill leading down to the village, and I recalled various scenes from *Doc Martin* as we wandered down the narrow lane of cottages and shops towards the harbour. I would not have been surprised if any of the main characters from the television series had suddenly come into view. The filming had certainly captured the essence of this village.

Having reached the harbour area, which is probably the only flat area in Port Isaac, we instantly recognised the pub where some of the scenes of the series were shot. Jon's tapeworm gnawed at his willpower, so in we went to let him order something with crab, or lobster, or both together. I didn't feel particularly hungry, and when I looked over the lunch menu, perhaps that was just as well; the prices were geared to the tourist trade stimulated by the television series. But it was pleasant enough just sitting in the famous pub and enjoying the atmosphere.

At one point, we started to consider what would be our best way of getting to Rock to board the ferry for Padstow. Although it was only 2pm, it would be impossible to cover the eleven or so miles over testing terrain if we stuck to the coast path. We didn't know if there would be a bus service that could get us to the ferry by 5pm, which was apparently the time of the last ferry, so we set off again up the steep hill to find a bus stop with a timetable. Jon had his iPhone with him, but we couldn't make any progress in trying to find out the bus times or the ferry times. What we found out from the bus timetable wasn't encouraging. The only bus going to Rock wouldn't get us to the ferry in time – what to do?

We felt sure that our best bet would be a local taxi, a great idea, but a non-starter. After asking some locals, it became evident that there weren't any taxi firms in the village. Did we have to accept defeat, or was there something we were overlooking?

Just at that moment, something remarkable happened. A people carrier drove past the bus stop and waited just opposite us while waiting to turn right to go down into the village. It appeared to be some type of community bus service. Jon ran over and asked the lady driver if she could take us to Rock. She wasn't sure but would drop off her passengers and come back up the village hill to see if she could do anything for us. Back she came, checked with her base to make sure that there weren't any urgent pickups waiting, and agreed to take us to Rock straight away.

We arrived in plenty of time to catch the 5pm ferry, but we also had time to look at the timetable and discover that the last ferry was at 6pm. Unfortunately, that extra time would still not have been viable for us to walk around the coast and get there in time. Had we not been able to cross the Camel River that evening, the alternatives were not attractive. The road back up the riverside to Wadebridge looked on the map to be uninviting and possibly a dangerous country road where drivers tend to speed along, even on blind bends. From Wadebridge, there would have been another eight or nine miles on a cycle track to get us to Padstow. Altogether, we would have had to walk nearly twenty miles. That would have made it far too late to get into the Youth Hostel, meaning that we wouldn't have got the meal that had been paid for, and we would probably have had to sleep like vagrants wherever we could find anywhere to rest our weary bones.

There was a bus service between Rock and Wadebridge but late into the evening. We would still have had all the other problems described in not being able to get to the Youth Hostel in time. But not to worry, our ferry had just docked at Padstow, and the prospect ahead was good; good, that is, as long as we settled for the bus service from Padstow to Treyarnon Bay. Again, the coast path was out of the question if we were to reach the hostel in time for the evening meal. My commitment to backpacking combined with camping was strengthening by the day!

The ferry took us across the wide river and right into Padstow. It didn't take us long to find the bus stop, but the number of people waiting for the bus looked ominous. The bus didn't arrive on time. After a further fifteen minutes of waiting, some of the people in the queue were becoming restless and concerned. A forward-thinking soul in the queue rang through to the bus office to find out what had caused the delay. It was apparently being caused by congestion on the roads due to the volume of traffic leaving the Royal Cornwall Show near Wadebridge. No further information was available at this time.

After a further twenty minutes of delay, another person rang the bus depot to be told that our bus had developed gearbox trouble and was being towed back to base. But there was also good news. A replacement bus was on its way to us. Within two minutes, the bus arrived to a great cheer from us all, and on we went towards our objective.

We arrived at Treyarnon Youth Hostel within about thirty minutes of the restaurant opening time. After a quick shower, down we went for the meal. Not only was the meal very good, but just outside the dining room, on an open-air stage, a Swedish band started playing, and although it was not my usual choice of music, I did enjoy their sound. Their female singer really sang with great feeling, and I wondered if I could take to this style of music after all. Jon loved this group and was so carried away that he bought me a beer: I will cherish that memory.

The day started to catch up with us as the evening progressed, so it was time to head for the dormitory for a good night's sleep. There were two other guys in the dorm, one being an outgoing talkative type, but the other one hardly spoke. Neither one snored, according to Jon, who found it difficult getting off to sleep. I must have dropped off as soon as my head hit the pillow; it must be our age difference or something.

Breakfast was a highly regimented system whereby every food item that was taken, and everybody who took it, came under close scrutiny. When I asked for a second cup of coffee, the lady serving me flinched dramatically with indignation. Now I know what Oliver Twist felt like when he asked for more gruel.

Jon received a phone call just after breakfast to tell him that Ken, his father-in law, had suffered a relapse during the night. Jon said that he would travel down the coast to Newquay where he could pick up a main-line train to Plymouth from where he would then be able to drive up to see Ken and the family.

I knew the coast path from Treyarnon to Newquay, and although it had some demanding sections in it, the potential for prolonged training wasn't the sort of ground that we could derive maximum benefit from. I decided to travel with Jon by bus to Newquay and then back to Plymouth by train. We used the time on the train to plan our next session the following month when we would trek the big and demanding route around the coast from Newquay to Penzance, a journey of eighty-three great training miles.

I think you will enjoy reading about the joys and trials of that walk and especially about some of the fascinating characters we met on our travels in deepest, strangest Cornwall. See you again in the next chapter for that training epic, our last major training session before setting off for Kilimanjaro.

FIFTEEN

It was nearly six weeks before our next scheduled training walk, and the time dragged. We both kept up our gym training in separate locations, and Jon came back to Plymouth about a month after travelling to Reading to see his family and London to see his father-in-law in hospital. His father-in-law's condition had stabilised, but he was still very ill.

Jon's retirement had not been easy for him so far, but the training walks helped him to settle into a diverting routine. He had enjoyed the walks down from Minehead to Treyarnon and was even able to laugh about some of his reservations concerning the accommodation we had already adventured into. The hostels weren't to his liking at all, and when I reminded him that we still had four more hostels to experience, he grimaced like a Labrador puppy being given its first bath.

The departure day eventually arrived, and we set off for Newquay by train from Plymouth. Blue sky and encouraging sunshine lifted our spirits; it was so exciting to be going back on the South West Coast Path again. This coastal walking really can become addictive because it is all about serendipity. I am constantly amazed by how each walk, even over very familiar ground, can be so fresh and different: the light on the seascapes, the rippling sea itself, the cloudscapes in their infinite patterns, the varying sounds of streams and rivers, the exuberant birdlife, the hedgerows at different times of the year, the fragrances of the gorse in flower, the people one meets and talks with, the weather in its tranquillity or turbulence, and perhaps most of all, the thoughts and reflections passing through the mind when it is not fully mindful of all these other things going on all around in every second. As the writer William Faulkner expressed it, '…walking in this way, in the NOW, open to the resonances of nature… is this not a form of prayer?'. I know the feeling, and it is not necessarily linked to a particular religion, or any religion at all, it is a life force open to anyone who gives themselves up to nature. This is endorsed by a fragment from a poem by Wordsworth:

'...*Nature never did betray*
The heart that loved her'

The train arrived in Newquay after the two-hour journey, and we were ready for what the day would bring. But the first event to happen to me that morning in Newquay wasn't what I expected, and it almost made me lose my usually controlled temper.

Because of our early start from Plymouth, breakfast had been simple, sparse, and rushed for both of us. We decided to pop into Wetherspoon to enjoy one of their breakfasts before setting out on the coast path for Perranporth. We had always enjoyed our visits to Wetherspoons, and the service is usually excellent. Jon went to the counter to order his while I found a table and kept an eye on our packs. It didn't take Jon long to get served, and there was no one else waiting to be served at the counter, so I expected to be back with Jon shortly.

A surly looking, unkept, middle-aged member or staff sauntered over to my end of the counter to take my order but suddenly changed his mind when a young lady who was apparently known to him came up to the counter from the main entrance. He made it quite obvious that his local favourites came first in his book, and if I didn't like it, then tough. I can overlook a lot of things but not outright ignorance. If only he had said to me that the young lady was probably in a rush, and if I didn't mind, he would serve her first, things would have been very different.

He started chatting to her about the local party scene in Newquay, but she pointed to me and said that she came in after me, and I was waiting to be served. This was ignored by the aging swinger.

"Get me your manager right this minute," I thundered to him. "If this is the way you usually treat customers, you shouldn't be customer-facing. Perhaps your manager will serve me in a more satisfactory manner."

This didn't have the effect I thought it would have. He came over to me in an aggressive way, and only when he could see that I would meet aggression with aggression did he start to falter and lose his confidence. The young lady beat a hasty retreat, probably fearing a nasty situation.

"Sorry to keep you waiting; didn't see you was there," he said in a much more conciliatory tone.

"That's fine, as long as we both know where we stand."

I ordered the breakfast and returned to join Jon.

"You were a long time."

"Yes, I had one or two problems at the counter, but I think it has all been resolved now." I kept my fingers crossed that the guy wouldn't sprinkle powdered glass on my scrambled eggs and beans on toast.

I saw that Jon, being a great detective, sensed that there was more in it than what I had glossed over. The incident left me disappointed with my behaviour in one way. I aspire to be a practitioner of the Stoic philosophy, and my reaction is probably not in the spirit of that body of teaching. Even so, I find it irksome to witness the sort of behaviour displayed by the gentleman in question, let alone being a recipient of such uncalled-for tantrums.

But at least I didn't continue to call for the manager and avoided putting the offender in a difficult position. Who knows what sort of life the man was living through and what had made him the way he was? As I pondered on these things, I felt annoyed that I had not behaved in the true stoic spirit, but I still felt that the outcome was a fairly satisfactory compromise. Knowing me as I do, I will think on the incident from time to time in an effort to extract a kernel of wisdom from it to help guide me in future.

* * *

We walked out of the restaurant and into a hazy sunlight doing its best to give a modicum of attractiveness to some of the seedy establishments we passed on our way down into the main town area. It was the week before the school holidays were about to start, but the town had already attracted many holidaymakers. Newquay is not everyone's ideal holiday resort, but the town did have a certain sparkle about it this day. In spite of that, as soon as we saw the far end of the town opening out into sand dunes, cliffs, and the big surfing beach of Fistral, we knew that our destiny that day lay right ahead towards the horizon, and the Perranporth Youth Hostel at the end of the rainbow. It was about twelve miles of reasonably easy going; just right for this shorter day of walking in view of the morning's train journey to get us to Newquay from Plymouth.

As we walked along the sandy path just above Fistral Beach, I remembered a Christmas and Boxing Day that Judith and I, and Judith's sister (Jon's mother) Vivien, had spent in the hotel just ahead of us at the far end of the beach. Considering the time of year, the weather on Christmas Eve when we arrived was quite warm and pleasant. The three days we spent at the hotel were good, and we gradually explored all around the immediate area. But the biggest surprise came on Boxing Day. The surfers were out in large numbers, and dozens of people started to take up their positions down on the beach from about mid-morning. By midday, barbeques were sizzling, dogs in their multitudes were drooling, beer was flowing, wine corks were popping, and everyone was having a great time. I was aware of the great Australian tradition of spending Christmas Day on the beach, but I never dreamed of this happening on this scale on a Boxing Day in England. Life is full of surprises!

Fistral Beach: a famous venue for international surfing competitions. The beach is west facing and is full on to whatever the Atlantic Ocean hurls at it.

We scaled the hill ahead and were rewarded with a striking seascape and a great-looking beach with the river Gannel flowing vigorously out over the sands of Crantock Beach to join the ebbing tide. It wasn't obvious to us then, but that river waited impatiently to throw a logistical problem at us.

After skirting the seawards end of Pentire, we found our way to the ferry service landing stage. The river was only a few yards wide at this stage of the tide, but frustratingly, the small boat ferry was nudged snuggly into the sand on the opposite bank at a point a little downriver and didn't show any inclination to return upriver to pick up more passengers, including us. I checked the map, and although we could get across the river by walking upriver for a way to the footbridge, the rumour circulated that the bridge was closed for repair. That would mean a considerably longer walk to a crossing point further upriver and then having to cover more ground to get back to the coastal path.

I studied the river as it flowed past the landing stage. Although the water was clear, its turbulence made it difficult to judge the river's depth at this point. Looking across at the opposite bank gave me the impression of relative shallowness.

"Jon, how would you feel about getting across commando style?"

"You cannot be serious," he let out in a disbelieving tone that reminded me of John McEnroe directing his sharp-edged disbelief at a tennis umpire.

"We can do this if we use our survival bags to keep the packs and gear dry. You are an outstanding swimmer. All we need to do is lower ourselves into the river and walk across, pushing the packs in front of us. If we wander into a deep channel between the sand banks, a few swimming strokes will get us over to the other side in no time. Admittedly, the sun isn't that prominent at the moment, but it is warm, and we can dry out quickly as we walk briskly along."

I have known Jon for a long time, but his face crinkled into an unfamiliar expression that seemed to suggest that I had finally lost it. He relaxed again after I said that I was only joking, but I had actually been tempted to give it a try.

Just as we were laughing about my little 'joke', the ferry started to make its way back over the river towards us. The ferryman helped two elderly passengers get out of the boat and then started to make the craft shipshape in a way that suggested the working day had ended. I asked him if he would take us to the other side before he packed up for the day. His expression spoke volumes. We were the only two people waiting to get across the river, and he could tell that he held all the cards.

"If you wait another thirty to forty minutes, the river will be low enough to wade across; it's dropping fast, but if you want me to take you over now at the end of a hard day, I will have to charge you £2.50 each. You can't expect me to charge the usual sixty pence if I'm on overtime."

I looked at Jon and smirked. We knew that he had us over a barrel of pilchards, and although we did have the option of taking the long detour, that wasn't appealing. We jettisoned our principles, accepted that we were in Cornwall and also accepted that we had met our match, and that's a lot to accept for me, who was born in Cornwall.

The rip-off journey across the river took all of thirty seconds, and the ferryman didn't even sing us a sea shanty to give us some value for our money, but I did see something interesting as the boat set out from the landing stage. The boat's sheltering influence smoothed out the surface of the river, and I could see that there really was a deep channel between the sand banks. Had we tried to wade across, we would have been out of our depth within about ten paces of the shore. Perhaps the £2.50 each was a good investment after all; perhaps that's why the ferryman stood expectantly as we clambered out of the boat. No! He didn't get a tip from us. It is said that sharks around the Cornish coast are nowhere near as plentiful as they once were. It is also said that the biggest sharks left in the area can sometimes be found running ferry services across some of the rivers, but perhaps that is a bit harsh. I am sure that many of these characters are honest and fair to their customers and to the taxman.

We walked across the wet sand to pick up the coastal path again, and we found it flirting with the sand dunes. There were plenty of surfers bobbing expectantly out on the generally small swell waves, but the odd tempting wave rose up, it seemed out of nowhere, to muster just enough power to launch them towards the beach. Yet it seems that it's still possible to have a good day's surfing without encountering the exciting power surging in with total focus from the Atlantic.

The headland of Pentire Point West bounded Crantock Beach. We rounded the headland, and the much smaller beach of Port Joke came into view. There must be an interesting story behind the naming of that beach, but I haven't been able to find out anything reliable about it.

Having stopped for a rest and to take in the view, I glanced over our map and was struck by the number of caravan and campsites that were scattered all around the area between Newquay and the area we were now in. I made a mental note of this in the event that I might want to backpack along this coast again at some stage. Wild camping is great, but it isn't always possible. And it isn't always possible to find a spring or stream to supply water for cooking and washing. Campsites usually provide all the basic facilities and are generally worth the overnight fee. One thing to be aware of is the typically steep increases in site fees during the high season when holidaymakers swarm into such places.

Another drawback of campsites for many lone backpackers is that they prefer the quietness and solitude of walking by themselves for long periods. This tends to be more the case as modern life closes in on us. Wild camping by oneself can be a great antidote to this. Watching the sun setting over a wonderful landscape or seascape can be pure bliss. To see the stars gradually appearing in the late evening sky is something that makes me feel at one with the whole universe. Do we have a spiritual dimension? I can remember lone backpacking trips when I thrilled to the profound feeling within me that there was no denying that we truly are, or have the potential to be, far more than the sum of our physical and mental make-up. Such contemplations are the occasional enchantments of backpacking alone. But, as the poet (Shelly) wrote:

'Rarely, rarely, comest thou,
Spirit of delight'.

"Here, get some of this down you," Jon offered, not realising just what a weird juxtaposition he had just created. He handed me a large hunk torn from a malt loaf. That brought me back to the present moment with a calorie-anticipating jolt.

We set off again across the sandy soil, along the coastal path. That path was beginning to be a metaphor picturing our journey through life. The sun had now powered its beams through the hazy sky, and it warmed us just enough to take away the earlier chill of the sea breeze.

I had never walked this area of the coast before, but as we rounded the headland of Kelsey Head, we saw another fine surfing beach that I recognised immediately; it was Holywell Bay. How did I know that beach as if I had been born and bred there? If you have followed the *Poldark* series on television, you too would recognise the two huge and magnificent pyramid-shaped rocky outcrops just offshore at the far end of the surf beach. They are called Carter's or Gull Rock and are frequently seen as a backdrop to the dramatic and enthralling stories that are being filmed on this beach as the Winston Graham novels about the impressive character of Captain Poldark, his loves, his family, friends, and various enemies unfold.

Holywell Bay isn't the only location for filming this great story, but it is one of the most striking of all the Cornish locations that are featured. It was fairly quiet on this day as we took in the rugged beauty of the place, but we later found out that on days of fine weather, especially at weekends, so many vehicles try to get down through the narrow country road approaching the beach that frequent gridlocks are a real headache. You can imagine the chaos caused when campervans travelling in opposite directions cannot pass one another in the narrow lane and with streams of other vehicles lining up behind, each one making it really tricky to reverse back to the nearest possible passing place. If you want to see such stunning places these days, it is best to backpack along the coast or visit out of the holiday season.

We walked the length of the Holywell Bay, not on the sandy beach but on the coast path just above as it scribbled its way over the sand dunes and coarse grasses. Penhale Point rose up in front of us with its disused mineshafts and the remains of an ancient settlement. But it was just as we rounded the point that Jon suddenly recognised where we were. It was the dismal and disused collection of old huts and storehouses known as Penhale Camp, surrounded by tall wire fencing encompassing many memories of servicemen sent here for training. In fact, Jon's first job was in the Ministry of Defence, and he was tasked on a number of occasions to deliver quantities of small arms and ammunition to Penhale Camp from the depot in Plymouth.

There is a poignant story in the camp's history during the Second World War. Penhale was one of the camps used to rehabilitate and update the training of troops coming back from the epic Dunkirk rescue mission. Penhale is just a short walk from the long, sandy, Perran Beach, and this must have brought back many dark thoughts of the suffering and death all around these survivors while being bombarded by German troops on the beaches of Dunkirk while awaiting their rescue. But as if this wasn't enough, something much worse lay in store for them.

On Sunday the 7th of July, 1940, twenty-three of these servicemen were killed when a lone German bomber flew over Penhale Camp and released its bombs. There were also many men who suffered serious injuries in the attack. This seems to have been the first air attack on Cornwall in that war, and it may be that the bomber pilot couldn't locate the small airfield that was his primary target and released his bombs as he flew over Penhale. What a cruel irony to escape from Dunkirk, only to meet a death like that on the north coast of Cornwall!

* * *

As we left Penhale Camp, the path took us above an awesome rock chasm. The sea around the coast was quiet, but the swell broke into this chasm with surprising force considering that the rock formation forming the chasm happened to be at right angles to the oncoming swell waves. I think the Romantic poets would have seen this as an example of the sublime, the raw power of nature.

We rounded Ligger Point and marvelled at the beauty of the huge expanse of Perran Beach at low tide, glistening its way towards Perranporth in the far distance. Yet another sight that confirmed for me the exhilaration of the trekking life with all its incredible beauty and serendipity!

Our path took us right down onto the dry, sandy beach, and we immediately felt the reduction in traction after being used to walking on the much harder ground of the typical terrain of the coastal path. We moved out from the dry beach, where the tide hadn't reached, onto wet sand where the tide had compacted it into a better walking surface. Far from being like a marine desert of pure tangy sand, there was an array of objects waiting to be spotted. Shells were there in abundance: crinkly scallop shells, twisty snail-like shells of various types and colours, razor clam shells with their sharp edges and muted but fascinating hues, shells that crabs had outgrown, decorated with barnacles like miniature volcanic cones; conical lug worm spores – even more like volcanic cones – formed as the burrowing worms forced the spoil heaps behind them as they excavated their shafts, small, sea-tormented pebbles that would have been significantly bigger thousands or millions of years ago before attrition had smoothed them and would keep on smoothing them until they too met their destiny and became minute grains of sand. But the most striking sight that day was the widespread marooning of small jellyfish along the whole length of the beach. Most of them were about two or three inches across and as smooth as if they had just been tipped out from a precision mould, their flying saucer shapes reflecting the strong sunlight. This beached armada of jellyfish just lay there across the whole of the two miles of this wonderful beach and was presumably waiting for the tide to refloat it and send it on its current-reliant way. I hope that I am right about them still being alive and waiting for the tide; if not, it would seem like a cruel trick of nature's tides to 'shipwreck' them and leave them to their doom.

As we drew nearer to Perranporth, surfers were out in big numbers. The map shows the designated surfing area as being within about three quarters of a mile of beach along from the town, and certainly it would be a bit of a struggle to walk much farther along the beach with the board and any associated gear for a good surfing session. The other thing about this Perranporth end of the beach on that particular day was that it had an exclusive area of tempting waves to thrill the more experienced surfers.

I drew my fascinated gaze away from the surfers and looked up to the top of the cliff face looming steeply in front of us. There, on the top of this cliff, called Droskyn Point, was our accommodation for the night. The sight of this hostel in its dramatic location sent a little quiver of excitement through me. It was very different from any other hostel I had seen, and it had something waiting for us that I will never forget.

Perranporth seemed like a lively little town, at least on this day, but in winter it must be a very different story. Jon's Achilles tendon injury had been giving him trouble since leaving Newquay, and it hadn't been tested by any really steep climbs along our route so far. But here, right at the end of the day, was a long, steep climb to get us to the hostel. We had planned to get settled in the hostel, have a shower, and then amble down into the town again to get a well-earned evening meal. Jon was in doubt whether it would be sensible for him to attempt this extra and demanding walking today in view of the injury, and by the time we reached the hostel, he had decided to rest that evening and try to give himself the best chance of being able to complete the next leg of our walk on the following day.

Our accommodation was in a six-berth dormitory, and there were two guys in residence when we arrived. I took a leisurely shower, and Jon encouraged me to go down to the town and have a good meal and perhaps a beer or two. He was quite happy to just rest on his bunk. I offered to bring him back something to eat, but he wasn't feeling hungry; that amazed and concerned me, knowing what an appetite he normally had. Time would tell if he really should attempt the big walk to Portreath on the following day. If not, we could at least pick up a bus in Perranporth to get us to the train station at distant Truro and then back to Plymouth. But it was too early to write off the walk at the moment.

The town buzzed with activity that evening, and I noticed that the surfers were still out in the bay squeezing every last second out of the lovely day. I decided on cod and chips for my meal and soon found a pleasant-looking restaurant. The place was quiet; in fact, I was the only customer in there. The meal ordered, I sat back and relaxed while it was being cooked. The waitress came back and explained that they were about to close, and I was the last customer of the day. There were two nice cod fillets left, and they could both be prepared for me if I was hungry, and the charge would remain as for just the one. My lucky day! Naturally, I left a healthy tip for the staff when I left.

As I walked around the town, an unaccustomed feeling of generosity came over me, and I decided to take back a small bottle of wine for Jon. I soon found a mini-market and bought us a bottle each. Jon is always talking about the great pleasures of sundowners, and our small hostel had a narrow but suitable garden between it and the edge of the tall cliff. I had noticed earlier that the sea view from the little garden offered a splendid spot for a sundowner as it had a great view of the setting sun; what more could we ask? Jon would undoubtedly love this idea and it would hopefully make him feel better.

I entered the dormitory, anticipating an enthusiastic welcome from Jon when I invited him to the sundowner, but the scene that greeted me was way beyond anything that I could have imagined. The two guys who had been there originally had gone out, and they had been replaced by two younger men in their late teens or early twenties.

There was a resolute sense of solemnity in the room, and the two lads were standing by Jon's upper bunk where he was still resting his leg. Jon seemed to have a mesmerised expression on his face, and I had never seen him looking so angelic before. Jon introduced me, and the lads invited me to join the three of them in prayer for Jon's leg injury. I was completely disoriented. The last thing I wanted to do at that moment was to look at Jon as I knew that once my giggling fit started, there would be no stopping Jon from joining in. With head bowed, eyes clamped tightly shut, and with a trembling throughout my taught body brought on by a Herculean effort to keep my composure, I gave every impression of having joined in the spirit of the prayer circle. Jon took me to task later on for going along with all this and leaving him out on a limb, but I explained that I thought this once-in-a-lifetime experience would take his mind off the pain of the injury. He remained very sceptical about my motives, bearing in mind that he had spent many years as a senior detective.

At the end of the short prayer, the lads wanted to know if the injury was feeling any better. Jon's faint praise for their efforts didn't satisfy them, and they explained to him with undeniable zeal that the time had come for the laying-on of hands so that the full power from above could flow through them into his leg. I knew instinctively that Jon would freak out at this approach, so I rapidly dived in with what I thought was a brilliant alternative plan.

"I'm really sorry, lads, but I promised Jon a sundowner for this evening. I brought the wine up from the town, Jon, and the light outside is already beginning to fade, so I think we had better make a move now before it is too late to catch the setting sun."

"Yeah, sorry about this, friends, but like he says, we have been looking forward to this all day. But thanks for your help with my injury; it's already feeling a lot better, should be fine for the morning."

Jon jumped from his bunk with an athletic flair, jammed his feet quickly into his trainers, apologised again to the bemused helpers, and skipped nimbly to the door with me in joyous pursuit.

When we were several yards down the corridor, Jon upbraided me in a semi-humorous way for going along with the prayer meeting with such apparent transcendence. I couldn't put up a defence because I was laughing so much that I just found it impossible to speak. By the time we reached the garden, the sun hadn't far to go before dipping into the horizon. It was that most heavenly of light as it enveloped Jon that he appeared almost angelic again in its beam, clearly a sign that something very special had infused him after his experience with the two lads. I thought it better not to joke with him about what I thought the sunlight on him was revealing to me; I didn't think that he had yet quite forgiven me. Having said that, after watching the sun dip down below the horizon, enjoying the wine, and finally accepting just how totally unexpected the whole thing was, Jon recovered from his experience and saw the funny side of his evening's departure from normality. The two lads were not in the dormitory when we returned, so we turned in and slipped away into a wine-friendly sleep, but not before I had to consciously suppress another fit of the giggles as the events of the evening flickered across my mind.

SIXTEEN

The next morning smiled its way into my consciousness, and I realised that Jon was calling to me that he had made coffee out in the kitchen. I washed rapidly and made my way to where Jon was sitting in the dining area talking to a young lady who had a dressing on her head. Jon introduced me, and I soon found out that the head wound had been caused by her surfboard flipping forcefully back at her as she became unbalanced on an awkward wave while surfing the previous day. She had been under instruction just off Perranporth Beach at the time, so a quick recovery was carried out by her instructor and two lifeguards. I think she was still in a certain amount of shock even as we were speaking. She started relating her recent life story with all the problems of disappointed love and being unable to settle down to anything yet after gaining her degree at Oxford. Although we were sympathetic to her predicament, the story was becoming more and more melodramatic, and we made our excuses to leave as I had booked us in for breakfast down in the town. We were certainly meeting some characters on this trip, but the most hypnotic of them all was going to happen later that morning when we met up with Avalon Alfie in St Agnes. Watch this space!

Breakfast was welcome and excellent. The beach cleaners were out early doing their bit for the town, and the weather suggested that there would be many visitors today. Some surfers lolled on their boards out in the lazy swell, but the absence of any waves to speak of didn't seem to worry them. It seems that the sea breezes often billow their way in when the sun warms the sea during the day, and the cooler air races in to take the place of the rising warmer air in a surfer and dinghy sailor preview of paradise.

We planned our day's walk before setting out from the restaurant. Our gear was back at the hostel where the staff kept an eye on it. This saved our efforts in carrying the packs down the hill and then all the way back up again to the hostel where the coast path passes just outside their door. A shop was open where we could buy some snacks for the day ahead as there weren't any other shops until we reached St Agnes. I had heard of St Agnes many times before but had never been there. The coastal route was about five miles in length, so it would be a convenient stopping point for a mid-morning coffee and perhaps a toasted teacake to keep us going until we reached our overnight accommodation in Portreath; yet another hostel!

As we were discussing hostels, Jon told me about his miserable night's sleep in the hostel we were just leaving. It seems that Jon's head was only about a foot from an Oscar-winning snorer who was also in a top bunk. The tops of their respective beds converged into a shared corner, and Jon estimated that he only managed an hour's sleep, if that. I didn't hear a thing, so I assumed that Jon's experience with the two lads had unsettled him and made sleeping doubly difficult. Recalling my warnings to Jon about some of the drawbacks of hostels, I asked him if he had reconsidered his anathema to camping if we take on any future trips. He repeated all his objections to camping in graphic, but unprintable, terms; having said that, I did detect a slight softening in his attitude following our recent hostel experiences. We only had three more hostels booked in, and that would take us to the end of our main Kilimanjaro training. I put this to Jon as gently as I knew how, but it didn't revive his spirits in any appreciable way; at least I tried.

We clambered up the hill back to the hostel to collect our gear, and Jon's Achilles tendon appeared to be holding up well. He would let me know if it seemed unwise to carry on, but so far so good. I had a well-stocked first aid kit with me, including some suitable bandages for strapping, if that seemed like a good idea. The pain killers could also be a good idea, so we were quite well prepared.

With packs strapped on, and ready for the day ahead, we set off on the path and looked forward to some more great landscapes and seascapes. It soon became clear that the landscapes were dismal. Derelict mine workings festered their way across the cliff tops and for quite a way inland as well. No birds sang here. No attractive coastal vegetation flourished here. The spoil heaps curdled and pitted the earth in battlefield fashion. Geology had been torn into with a furious drive for profit. But one person's profit is another person's slender means of subsistence. Miners had lived, struggled, and often died in such devastation of the natural world. Families relying on them must have lived fraught lives of worry and scarcity, but the likelihood of miners finding better work was slim indeed.

This incredibly unattractive landscape was one thing, but the seascape made up for it on this morning of sunlight and dramatic coastline. We were also looking forward to passing through St Agnes, now not far ahead along the path.

The path took us down into the little town, and it looked attractive and welcoming. A tea garden appeared as we explored the area close to the small beach, and we both nodded in agreement that this would be ideal for our mid-morning break. It had a large sitting out area with several tables available. But the striking thing about the counter and food preparation area was that it was a beautifully converted container unit, the type that you see in great layers stacked on the decks of ocean-going container ships, plying ceaselessly between China and the rest of the world.

Jon found a table in a good location while I went to order the coffees and chocolate brownies for energy. Very few people were in the tea garden at this stage, and it was so pleasant that we decided to just take our time and enjoy the laidback atmosphere. We only had about another ten miles to travel that day to get to the hostel, so there was no rush whatsoever.

I hadn't had an opportunity to see much of the beach as yet, but I didn't want to drag Jon down there if he would rather just sit in the garden for a while or just press on with the walk again. Just at that moment, his mobile rang with a call coming in from one of his daughters. I could sense from Jon's face and tone of voice that this was another complicated teenage situation welling up for him to advise on. It would be unusual for this kind of call to be wound up in anything less than about twenty minutes, so I signalled to him that I was going down to the beach to take some photographs.

I had almost reached the beach area when a local gentleman, who was standing by a car, called out to me that my Nikon camera looked really good. We exchanged some opinions about 'real' cameras. "Not the sort," he said, "that you find embedded in phones these days." Then he went on to tell me that he had lived in St Agnes all his life and that back in his younger days, he made good money selling pictures of surfers riding the waves off the local beach. His collie dog nuzzled me, and I just had to make a fuss of him.

"My name's Alfie, what's yours?"

"Eric. What's the dog called? Oh! Rover, great name."

"Now, can I ask a favour of you?"

Here we go, I thought. *Now what?*

"I've just been given these books here in the back of my friend's car, but my car's over yonder in the car park by the tea garden. Rover is pretty good, but I have to keep him on a lead near these roads. He's got no sense where roads are concerned. Could you help me to get the books over to my car? I would be very grateful."

"Yes, certainly, Alf. Do you do a lot of reading?"

"No, these are for my mother. She loves reading."

We made our way over to the car park with me carrying the two boxes of books, and all the while Alf was asking me about the walk I was on. I briefly explained that I was training with Jon with the intention of climbing Mount Kilimanjaro in two months' time. He was impressed. We had just reached the car park, and I waved to Jon. Alf shouted over to greet Jon like a long-lost friend. Jon's expression said it all. He rapidly concluded that I had met an old friend in the most unlikely of places. Alf and I walked over to the tea garden, with Alf clearly very keen to meet Jon.

Alf introduced himself before I had a chance to get a word in, and I could tell that Alf's quite overpowering charisma had temporarily disoriented Jon who was still at a loss as to how I came to be carrying two heavy boxes for Alf in the first place. I didn't get an opportunity to explain how all this came about until we were leaving the town. Alf insisted on telling Jon all about the history of St Agnes. There were the Vikings who discovered that this area had wonderful deposits of copper, top-quality tin, and other valuable metals. History took a lot of twists and turns at this point when Alf (who had Jon bemused and transfixed, like the wedding guest in Coleridge's *Ancient Mariner*) proclaimed that it was this discovery that started the Bronze Age (?).

Alf then led us into the historical labyrinth of King Arthur. We learnt that, if I followed this correctly, St Agnes was in all likelihood, Avalon, a Celtic paradise where the Knights of the Round Table lived an exciting life rescuing fair maidens and killing dragons. Alf was in doubt whether Tintagel or Camelford was the ancient site of the Round Table. I suppose it is good to leave a bit of room for doubt!

Jon's face expressed that he was stunned by this totally unexpected event that had taken us hostage. I was struggling for the second time in two days to control a giggling fit. My only recourse was to turn around to Rover, who lurked just behind me, and make a fuss of him with my body bent over and my near-hysterically contorted face out of sight.

At this point, Jon used all the self-control and assertiveness built up over his thirty years of policing to break free of Alf's hypnotic effect over us. It wasn't easy. Alf was in full flow, and he was still talking consummately as we left the table in the tea garden to escape.

Just as we reached the gate to leave the garden, we spotted that there were several people watching us from the low perimeter wall. They broke into spontaneous applause. I spoke briefly to one of the audience and found out that the applause came from locals who had seen Alf in action many times before. Apparently, we had done very well indeed to escape within fifteen minutes as some visitors had been held hypnotically for a lot longer. It seems that Alf is a bit of a joker. In any event, the laugh was on us this day, but it was an experience that I will treasure for a long time.

* * *

Chapel Porth Tin Mine. This part of Cornwall is studded with imposing mine buildings of this type

The next section of coast more than made up for the disappointing scenes we encountered earlier that morning when we left Perranporth. Instead of ravaged coastal landscapes, we now had a vista across a wide sweep of bay, and in the foreground, there was a dramatic mine building rising up out of the glorious colours of the surrounding heather. This, as far as I could tell, was called Chapel Porth, but there seems to be some local disagreement about this name:

I looked out towards the horizon, and the sunlight mirrored our mood in the scintillating, playful way it sparkled across the whole expanse of the sea. It brought back to my mind the play that we had recently been unwitting participants in when we found ourselves under the sparkling spell of 'Avalon Alf' in St Agnes. Gentle breezes caressed the heather, and the thrift plants waved their welcome to anyone who had the good fortune to be here in this lovely spot on such a day. Surely, backpacking in this weather with such uplifting scenery has to be one of the outstanding joys of life!

We gradually made our way over good walking terrain towards Porthtowan, which has yet another good surfing beach. Our next point of interest on the map was a cove with the ambiguous name of Sally's Bottom. I wondered why it had been named in such a way. Local history is certainly a fascinating subject, especially in Cornwall!

There were about another five miles to travel before reaching our day's destination of Portreath, and the sun beat down on us to test our resolve. We eventually arrived in the town, and it was quiet. There had been no earlier opportunity to shop for food for the next day's breakfast, but we came across a mini-market in the town that was well-stocked. It was while we were shopping that the thought suddenly crossed our minds that the hostel looked too far away inland from Portreath to make it viable for an evening meal. Accordingly, we stocked up on some standby rations just in case there wasn't anywhere convenient to get our meal that evening.

The map showed that the hostel nestled in a rural area about two miles up through the woodland running along the valley east of Portreath. Our map happened to be large scale, but it was not particularly clear as to which way we should leave the town in order to get onto the correct path. I asked a young couple who were passing us near the edge of town for the best route to take for the hostel. They had never heard of a hostel in this vicinity but suggested that if it existed, it would be along the country lane rising up the hill just ahead. We set off on that route but without feeling very confident about those directions.

After a mile or so, we began to get that uncertain feeling, and at the same time, we started to trust our instincts more. At this point, a little family group came along the lane from the opposite direction. We asked them for directions and found that, although we could have reached the hostel eventually on this path, it would be better to walk back into the town and take the country lane by the river. This would take us into Illogan woods, and when we came to a fork in the woodland path, we should take the left side. They seemed confident in their directions, so we thanked them and backtracked to the town and hopefully onto the right path for the hostel.

It had been a hot and enjoyable day; however, we were now beginning to feel weary. The cool of the wood helped, but the path seemed to go on and on without a clue to encourage us that we were anywhere near civilisation. Eventually, we came to the fork in the path and went left, as advised. Soon after that, we came to a small sign directing us to the hostel at Nance, and about time too!

The hostel rose up in front of us, and it looked pretty appealing, even to Jon, who, as you know, wasn't a keen visitor to hostels. The thought of a cool shower, an even cooler beer, and perhaps a good meal out this evening persuaded the life to flow back into us.

Unlike most Youth Association Hostels, this one was privately owned and run by the farming family who lived in the large farmhouse just across the way. The lady of the house came out to welcome us when we arrived and gave us a quick guided tour of the place. The dorm that we had been assigned to was equipped with several beds and no bunks. There happened to be a young Indian man in the dorm when we entered, and the lady of the house introduced us. He had recently taken up a technical job in Truro, which is quite a drive away. Although the commuting was demanding, he could at least stay at the hostel while viewing properties closer to his place of work. This represented a considerable saving in cash for him, and it would certainly help with all the costs of buying a house and fitting it out to his own liking.

Jon asked him about the various people he met who were passing through this way and stayed for a while at the hostel. He had seen several people over the past three weeks since becoming a resident here, but the majority were not walking as we were but were using the hostel as a base for walking or just sightseeing. Most of them came by car. This hostel really was quite different from the ones that we had stayed in so far on this trip. But if we thought that this hostel was different, we were in for a shock the following night in St Ives.

We managed to get a good meal in a pub that was down in a hamlet about three fields away, but at least it was a pleasant evening for a walk in the country and quite a change from the coast.

Later that night, I unknowingly caused a situation back in the dorm. Jon, not being a good sleeper, suddenly became aware of a figure standing at the foot of my bed in the near darkness of the night. Not only that, but he was pleading with my sleeping figure to 'please, please, please stop snoring'. It was our Indian friend who needed his sleep to face a demanding day ahead of him. Jon called him over and explained that snoring had to be accepted in such communal settings. Jon should know after his shocking experience of the snoring from the world-class exponent during the previous night's wrecked sleep in the Perranporth hostel. Jon calmed our friend down and advised him to just shut the noise out of his mind or go down to the kitchen and brew a mug of coffee. The poor guy went back to bed and apparently eventually drifted into a compromised sleep. When I greeted him the following morning, he wasn't his usual chirpy self, and I assumed that he just wasn't a morning person. Being a circumspect sort of guy, I didn't reiterate the point to Jon, when he later explained what had happened, that camping is usually the better option from many points of view. But hostels are great if you camp in their grounds and use their drying room facilities, the kitchen, the showers, and if they offer them, an evening meal and breakfast. Not only is the price attractively lower, but you can normally ensure a snore-free zone, tempting, or what?

Jon surprised me by having our scrambled eggs and beans on toast all ready when I finished shaving and appeared in the dining room. The fact that he is growing a beard in true, male mountaineer style gave him the extra time to do all this for us, and I really appreciated it. In fact, I was so surprised and grateful that I volunteered to make the coffee.

We were well organised and set off from the hostel in good time. The two-mile walk back through the woods to Portreath would give Jon the opportunity to assess his Achilles tendon problem. In the event, it wasn't too bad and certainly better than it had been for the past two days. As we walked down through the woods, our talk naturally centred on the day's journey to St Ives. I suggested that in view of the mainly undulating terrain on the route, the lack of good hill-training prospects, we should take the opportunity to have a more restful day and travel to St Ives by bus. Not only would this help to rest Jon's injury in preparation for the final two days of very hard walking, but we could take advantage of the weather in St Ives to relax in the interesting old fishing town with its undeniable atmosphere and interesting restaurants and pubs. I knew that Jon would run with that idea, but I had another feature of the town in reserve. Today was Thursday, the day of the regular St Ives Farmers' Market in the town's guildhall. I had been to the market twice before and clearly remembered the delicious food on offer in the cafe run by the farmers' wives. The array of home-grown and home-cooked food on offer made me feel hungry just thinking about it, and I knew that Jon's tapeworm would pummel him into willing submission, and so it was when I described the treat just waiting for us later in the morning.

A quick check of the bus times showed that we had about an hour to wait before the next bus for St Ives would arrive. There was a pleasant-looking coffee house nearby with a small area of seating outside where we could sit and enjoy our coffee in the morning sun. After finishing my coffee, I decided to go for a stroll around the small harbour. Jon opted to stay and read his newspaper, but just as I was setting off on my walk, he impressed upon me to guard against picking up any more strangers like 'Avalon Alf'. I responded to that comment by reminding him that backpacking was all about serendipity, and he should prepare to be surprised by the unexpected. He was still shaking his head and tut-tutting as I walked away with a broad smirk of devilment on my face.

The harbour dozed in the morning's lovely sun; portly seagulls preened themselves on the rooftops and bollards; smells of fish and fishing gear infused the whole area; a few locals loitered by the boats; children tried to tempt crabs onto their baited lines; women with baskets of groceries chatted in small jovial groups; and the whole area resembled a series of scenes ready and waiting for the artist's first brushstroke to capture this essence of a Cornish fishing village on a glorious summer's day.

I made my way back to where Jon was still studying the sports pages of his daily paper. The time had passed quickly, and we only had ten more minutes to wait for the St Ives bus. As we walked up to the bus stop, the bus we wanted drove right past us without stopping. We were just in the middle of venting our disgust about being left high and dry when the bus came rattling back up the road again, and it soon became clear that the driver had merely driven straight down to the turning point as there wasn't anyone to drop off at our stop. All was tranquil again until we entered the bus. I entered first and produced my bus pass. Jon's face puckered and wrinkled into something resembling the skin of a sun-dried prune as he choked back his indignation and dug deep into his reluctant pocket for the few pounds needed to get him to St Ives. It didn't help when I pointed out that it was a splendid day, and he should put material concerns to the back of his envious mind. Clearly, I will have to buy him a drink or two when we reach St Ives in order to curry favour with him again. Life surely is like a social minefield, is it not?

The journey to St Ives flashed scenically by the windows as the bus rattled along the blossom-filled country lane towards the town of Hayle. Glimpses of shimmering seascapes flickered into and out of view with hypnotic speed, and I knew that we were in for a great day of near-tropical weather in St Ives. We could spend the whole day in the town just relaxing and taking in the sights of summer along the massively popular old fishing harbour and beaches. It is a place of holiday dreams, but the right weather for its enjoyment is obviously important.

Our bus veered around into St Ives Bay as we started the downhill approach to the old town of Hayle, a town vastly different to St Ives but popular with holidaymakers at this time of year. The town was crowded today, and the build-up of traffic slowed our bus down considerably.

Once through the town, the speed picked up again, and it wasn't long before St Ives came into view. I reflected on the many times I had visited this place and how each time it loomed up before me, the excitement surged into me like a big incoming tide rushing in over a great expanse of glittering sand. Perhaps this is a sign that we would be deeply happy if Judith and I moved to St Ives from Plymouth to spend the rest of our lives living here. You may have experienced a similar power when you resonate to a particular place or opportunity. It can be something so strong that it feels like a guiding force in your life. Anyway, let's find out if the town and harbour still had its charm and magic; the same magnetic pull that has drawn so many fine artists to this place to live and work since the nineteenth century.

***

The bus pulled into the bus station at the top of the steep hill above the main town. Off we leapt, just glad to be out in the invigorating fresh air again after our journey from Portreath. The gulls calling overhead were the first sounds I registered, and next came the sea smells drifting up from the fishing harbour. The sea itself was sparkling and tropical in colour; we were lucky indeed with the weather. Having spent a week here once in bad weather, I knew what a difference it can make to a visit or holiday.

Jon had been here before when he was in his very early teens. Judith and I brought him down with us, and I distinctly remember a few tantrums. I am pleased to say that his outbursts are far less frequent these days, and he was behaving himself today... so far!

We pulled on our packs and headed down into the town to find our accommodation. This was another hostel, but instead of being run by the Youth Hostel Association, it was a privately owned and run hostel. I had never stayed in a private hostel before, and the prospect of experiencing the differences from the hostels we had stayed in so far on this trip was intriguing us both.

It didn't take long to find the place as it was conveniently just off the main part of the town. The front entrance opened onto a steep stairway that led up to the reception and lounge area that was light, bright, and airy. Our welcome was warm and welcoming. We registered our presence, took a seat, and the owner brought us coffee and biscuits on the house. He stayed chatting with us for half an hour about our travels and also about some of the people who had visited the hostel. All of this was quite different from the hostel experiences we had come through in the past few weeks. It wasn't that the other hostels were lacking in the basic comforts, but this one felt more homely and relaxing, but was it too early to judge? Time would tell.

We had booked into a dorm for this visit as there weren't any private rooms. With coffee finished, we picked up our keys and made our way to dorm number six. It wasn't a bad room. There were six bunks, and, so far, we seemed to be the only two in residence. Having secured our gear in the lockers provided, we thought it was an ideal time to head over to the farmers' market for lunch. Just then, as we were passing through the reception area, Jon's mobile rang. It was another apparently intractable teenage problem to wrestle with, and Jon flopped back into an armchair with a look of theatrical desperation on his face. Within moments, he signalled to me that we would need to delay the visit to the market for about fifteen minutes. I quite understood and went back to the dorm to pick up a book from my pack.

As I reached the top of the stairs, the doorbell rang. I could see that the manager was tied up on the telephone, and with no one else immediately available, I went down the stairs to open the door for whoever was trying to come in. It was a young lady in her late twenties with a huge suitcase and an expensive-looking camera. She had just arrived by train and was already booked in here at the hostel. She had dragged her case from the station, and that would have been a great effort. Being a gentleman of the old school, I lifted the case to take it up the steep stairs for her. The weight nearly killed me, but I managed to haul it to the top and into the reception area where Jon was just finishing his call. The new guest thanked me for my efforts, and Jon and I then left for the market, not realising that we were in for a shock as the day wore on.

The town had started to get busy, and the farmers' market was bulging with customers. It trades in the town's guildhall, so even in wet weather it still goes ahead. We did a rapid circuit around all the stalls, and then went quickly to the magnificent food stall for lunch. What an astonishing array of locally produced food! Jon's face glowed with anticipation, and I could just imagine his tapeworm jumping for calorific joy. Flans, cheeses, smoked fish, slices of ham, chicken, beef, aromatically spiced vegetables and pasta, pies and pasties that one could imagine were baked in the farmer's wife's Aga cooker with her Labrador, the pride and joy of her kitchen, watching and waiting with practised hyper-focus. Cakes, scones with home-made jam and Cornish clotted cream, buns of many types, chocolate brownies, shortbread, fruit tarts, Victoria sponges generously embellished with strawberry jam and butter cream, all waiting to feed two hungry pilgrims who just happened to arrive in town by bus that morning.

With piled plates, we found a nearby table in the improvised dining area and tucked into a truly memorable lunch. It was difficult wrenching ourselves away from the jolly atmosphere of the market, but we were eager to look around the town and its beaches in this lovely summer weather. True to my word, I paid for both magnificent lunches in view of the promise I had made to myself to make amends for rubbing in the fact that Jon had been paying out quite a lot of money in bus fares during our journey down from Minehead. I think Jon was a little taken aback at this, and so he should have been at such a splendid show of generosity and conscience!

The town hummed with activity as holidaymakers and day trippers descended in swarms into the old town. The weather had certainly warmed up, so we decided to pay a quick visit back at the hostel to collect our sun hats and water bottles. I turned the key to open the door of room number six, and Jon entered first. His voice had a tone in it that I had never heard before.

"Sorry, but you are in the wrong room," Jon's shocked and strangely high-pitched voice bounced around the hard surfaces of the dorm.

"Is this room six?" asked a familiar voice just as I entered.

"Yes, but this is a men's dorm. There is some mistake here, and we had better sort this out at the reception desk."

The young lady, whom I had assisted with her large case earlier, smiled her recognition at me and went on to explain to Jon that this was a mixed-dormitory hostel. She asked Jon if that would be a problem, and after a long and tense moment of hesitation – and not wishing to sleep out on the streets of St Ives that night – he answered that if that was the usual procedure then there was no problem as far as he was concerned. I also agreed that it would not be a problem, and our initial shock and awe dissolved into conformity.

The young lady was just changing out of her travelling clothes as we walked into the room, so we hurriedly picked up the gear we needed and sped out of the dorm in dazed disbelief. I had no idea that such hostels existed in the UK, although I was aware that mixed hostels were becoming increasingly common in Europe. Jon's ashen face needed the radiant sunlight out under the beautiful Cornish skies to restore his tanned equilibrium. We also both badly needed a beer or two to settle us down after that bolt from the disorienting blue. I suddenly thought ahead to what the camping arrangements might be on the trek up Kilimanjaro. If the tents were for four or six people, could it be that we would have to get used to mixed accommodation arrangements on the mountain? By the time we were on our second pints of 'Proper Job' ale, thoughts like these vaporised away like an early morning sea mist floating up from the ocean's placid surface.

Feeling relaxed, we cruised around the town until we found a suitable restaurant for our evening meal. We settled on the dining room above the Sloop pub. I had enjoyed a meal there before with Judith, and the harbour views were attractive in the early evening light. This would be fitting, as on the following day we would have our final evening meal at the hostel near St Just where I had stayed back in April when our group from the gym did this same two-day walk that Jon and I planned to begin tomorrow right after breakfast. The hostel meals weren't too bad at all, but it was not like having a meal in a good-quality restaurant. The evening following our stay at St Just, we wouldn't arrive at Penzance until mid-to-late evening, so our best bet then might be to get some fish and chips to eat while covering the last section of the walk to the Penzance train station. So, our meal that evening in St Ives would celebrate the training we had done over the 233-mile route from our starting point at Minehead to St Ives. The remaining forty miles to Penzance were the tough two-day trek described earlier. Having said that, each time I walk that section it seems so different from every other time that I have walked those ancient cliff paths.

We continued our walk around bustling St Ives and soaked up the bracing atmosphere of the place. There were the constant calls of the seagulls, the briny smells wafting up from the breaking wavelets as they rolled into the beaches, lobster pot smells interwoven with the fresh fish smells being unloaded in the harbour, the endless streams of visitors dressed in every colour you could imagine cascading out of narrow lanes and along the harbour front, several of them clutching their Cornish pasties as they trundled along. I bent down to take up a handful of fine sand from the harbour beach and then let it trickle through my fingers like the sand of an hourglass slowly releasing its embedded seconds and minutes to stream smoothly through the narrow waist of its tiny universe. And how many seconds and minutes and aeons had it taken for the sand's parent rock to split and divide, split and divide, split and divide to become sea-smoothed until these miniature specks of rock could form this lovely smooth beach?

My geological and temporal reverie was shattered in the next nanosecond. There was an explosion of volcanic anger right next to us. I looked up just in time to see a well-fed seagull making off with most of the pasty that a furious man had just started to eat. The red-faced man screamed abuse and shook the small remnant of pasty that he still clutched in his hand, as the smug seagull did a low flypast over his head. If the gull had performed a victory roll, I wouldn't have been surprised, such were its panache and aerial terrorism. The seagull's final triumph was an ear-splitting shriek to its nearby gang, as if to tell them, 'what fools these mortals be', as the spirit, Ariel, proclaimed to his master, Prospero in Shakespeare's *The Tempest*. As for Jon and I, we were aching with laughter but not within earshot of the poor victim who was still in an inconsolable rage. I dreaded to think what the robbed man would have done to the poor seagull had he been able to catch it!

We were still laughing as we walked over to Porthmeor surf beach. There was the glorious Tate St Ives art gallery perched above the sunlit beach like an eagle surveying the shimmering horizon, still as I remembered the scene from when I last visited with the other six gym members back in April before our two-day walk to Lamorna. The beach was alive with colourful surfboards, wetsuits, swimwear, and beach shelters of all sizes and shapes. Porthmeor's famous surfing waves were only making a token effort today, just enough to occasionally lift a board and surfer into a short skim along the glittering surface of the sea, but there were so many people splashing about in the water just off the beach that the surfers had to be ever watchful.

Time was moving on, so we dragged ourselves away from Porthmeor's swarming centre of activity with all of its movement and light and its aromas of barbeques and suntan lotion breezing in from the now-crowded beach. We decided to head back to the hostel for a quick shower and change of clothing ready for our stroll over to the dining room above the Sloop pub, apparently a favourite haunt of the old fishermen with their tales of huge catches of pilchards and mackerel and the wild gales they came through and survived to fish another day to drink many more pints in their favourite pub. It was a hard life, as the marvellous St Ives Museum makes abundantly clear.

Quietness pervaded the hostel when we arrived. The dorm was empty and with no sign that anyone else had yet been assigned to our room. We left again after a shower and change of clothes and headed out for our evening meal. I didn't think I would need another meal today after such a great lunch at the farmers' market, but the walking and fresh air of the long afternoon had persuaded me that a leisurely light meal and glass of wine could be a good idea.

We arrived back at the hostel just as the sun had set and made our way to the room. Jon hadn't mentioned the young lady again, but I could tell that his thirty years in the police had made him cautious of the situation we found ourselves in.

Justine was already in bed and peacefully reading. After exchanging hellos, it was time to undress and get into our bunks. Justine considerately drew her bed curtain, and everything went smoothly. There wasn't any problem whatsoever, but I wondered how I would feel as the only guy sleeping in a shared room with five or six young women. This was certainly a novel experience!

There was only one problem that night, and that just happened to be the constant 'chattering' and squawking among the seagulls who were apparently roosting right overhead on the roof, as well as on neighbouring roofs. It took some getting used to. The seagulls in our area at home seem to fly off into the twilight to sleep elsewhere; I hadn't appreciated just what a blessing that was until undergoing this St Ives experience. Although I eventually fell asleep, the seagull serenade started again at the crack of another superb dawn.

We had decided to have breakfast at the same nearby Wetherspoon restaurant that our 'magnificent seven' had visited back in April. After a quick wash and shave, and with rucksacks packed, I noticed that Justine was getting her camera gear ready for a day of photography in St Ives. I chatted to her briefly about some of the things that puzzled me with my new digital camera, and she was able to explain away the problems in an expert fashion. It transpired that she was a photojournalist. I wished that had been known the day before, as it would have been really something to talk with her about illustrating articles and features with well-spotted photographic opportunities.

We said our goodbyes and headed out for breakfast. The day held out plenty of promise for good weather, and the seagulls were still greeting the day that held out such promise for raids on unsuspecting visitors ambling down by the harbour with no inkling of what awaited them as they carelessly tried to consume their fish and chips, ice creams, and pasties.

With breakfast completed, we made our way along by the harbour beach and then over to Porthmeor surf beach. The beach was much quieter now than during the afternoon before when it swarmed with colourful humanity seeking happiness under the sun. This morning there were just a few people on the beach. Three guys were working over different parts of the big beach with metal detectors, heads down, shoulders slouched over, meditative in their demeanour, and ever-hopeful of finding the odd pound coin or perhaps a Rolex watch or two! Labradors scampered; two surfers slowly made their way out through the lazy wavelets; a jogger signatured his 'Man Friday' presence in the wet sand behind him; two lovers lingered languidly by the tideline, at least until a sea-drenched Labrador came over and shook a lavish quantity of the Atlantic over them. Everything was right with the world, and life was good. The start of the coastal path appeared a short distance ahead, and the promise of an excellent day's walk filled us with optimism that this penultimate day of training would be memorable. And it certainly was, but not in the way we imagined.

SEVENTEEN

All the old memories of this part of the walk came teeming back into my mind as we started out on the pathway. Could it really be forty or so years since I first set out to explore this wonderful part of England? No wonder its fame has spread and has now been recognised as one of the world's outstanding walking trails.

Jon's injury seemed to be much improved since yesterday morning, and the rest day in St Ives had been a great idea for both of us after our long, hot trek down from Newquay. The countryside basked in the morning sun, and the coastal scenery began to shimmer in the increasing, but pleasant, heat.

As the conditions might tempt adders to seek out the warm soil of the coast path, in order to coil up to absorb the heat of the sun, I reminded Jon of this and counselled caution, especially if we had to push through sections of path where we couldn't always see clearly along the path ahead. But the splendid morning made it difficult to really imagine that anything untoward could happen to either one of us.

I gazed out over the blue of the sea and the way it lightened in colour as it pulsed and rippled gently towards the horizon to merge with the summer sky. Some inshore fishing boats were out from St Ives, presumably after mackerel, or crab and lobster. A number of seagulls had started to follow one of the boats and were ducking and diving in an effort to scoop up whatever it was that had been thrown over the side by one of the crew. This is typical of what happens when crab and lobster pots are being hauled in, cleared of their catch, and freshly baited before being sent down into the depths again to tempt more shellfish. What remained of the older bait would be thrown over the side. Clearly, not only would the seagulls relish this, but unwary pasty-eating visitors ambling alongside the harbour and in the old lanes of St Ives might have an easier time of it with fewer seagull bandits waiting for a chance to swoop down for a tasty snack.

I looked up from my musings to see that Jon had drifted ahead of me by about fifty yards. He suddenly shrieked in anguish.

Oh no! I thought, *he's been bitten by an adder.*

Jon had doubled over to grab his leg, and the situation didn't look at all good. I ran forward as fast as I could with the pack bouncing on my back. He was in obvious pain, and as I ran, my mind raced through the limited options we had for treatment.

As I reached him, he was still holding his leg and seemed to be in agony. Then I saw a small, lifeless creature lying on the path alongside Jon's left foot. It wasn't a snake; it was a young stoat. It had shot out of the cover on the side of the path right on the spot where Jon's right boot had almost reached the ground where the little stoat had cowered, transfixed like a rabbit in a car's headlights. Jon had twisted back onto his left leg, and as he had desperately tried to steady himself, the stoat had sped forward right under the left boot as it came down heavily to the ground. The poor thing had been killed outright.

Jon was badly upset by this. He is an animal lover, as am I, and the whole incident noticeably affected him for the rest of the day. But there's more! With the violent twisting and desperate attempt to avoid treading on the poor stoat, Jon's Achilles tendon had been wrenched back into acute pain once more. He took a few paces forward to gage the extent of the injury. Walking was possible but by no means comfortable. Jon is tough and wanted to press on with the walk to St Just. I put it to him that if the long and demanding day's walk ahead of us did more harm than good, the Kilimanjaro trek could be put in jeopardy; not a welcome prospect for us. Jon agreed that if the pain became too bad, we would definitely find an escape route onto the main coastal road where transport could be picked up eventually to get us to either St Just or back to St Ives. I kept my fingers crossed that he would be all right as the day progressed.

We plodded on towards Zennor, and Jon's walking gradually became easier again. From Zennor, we forged on towards Pendeen Watch lighthouse and almost reached it by late afternoon. That was good going for someone carrying an injury like Jon's. But by this time, it became clear that it would be pushing things too far if we tried to walk the whole distance to the hostel at St Just. According to the map, there was a public path heading inland across some fields in the direction of Pendeen Village where we could pick up the bus service to St Just. From there, it was only a relatively short hike to the hostel. I explained to Jon that in about another half a mile, there was also a country lane running from Pendeen Lighthouse back to Pendeen Village. It tended to be fairly busy with visitors' vehicles this time of year, so the field path shortcut seemed like a better option for us. I had never walked that path, but it did look like a shortcut on the map, so off we went, through a battered gate that was reluctant to open fully for us, and headed along what was only a barely visible hint of a pathway.

The path suddenly disappeared altogether, so our best option seemed to be straight ahead in the general direction of Pendeen Village. It wasn't long before a strange structure appeared on our chosen route. It was a large drystone wall enclosure forming what looked like a small field within the field we were walking through. There were no access points visible from our angle, so we presumed that its entrance would be within the walls facing away from us.

We ambled up the sloping field until we came within view of the enclosure's far wall. A casual glance showed that this odd structure did have an entrance in that wall, and we gradually reached an angle where we could see clearly inside it.

"Bloody hell! Keep facing them, but walk backwards towards the nearest hedge. Now!" Jon did this immediately.

The two mean-looking bulls in the enclosure were no more than a hundred yards from us, with a wide-open gate inviting them to do what bulls sometimes do. Our nearest escape route was to reach the hedge about two hundred yards away and hope that we could scamper high enough up the hedge to avoid those massive horns. The big worry was Jon's leg problem in the event that we might have to make a sudden dash for it to outpace the bulls. I had both of my Nordic walking poles in my hands, but what good they would do against an attacking bull, I had no idea.

Both bulls had moved up to the open gate to glare at us by the time we had reached a safe distance from them, and we breathed easily again. But it does drive home the message that these dangers come out of nowhere.

"Well, we did it, Jon, and the good news is that we won't be confronted by bulls on our way up Kilimanjaro. Leopards maybe, or perhaps snakes on the first day's trek up through the rainforest, maybe even the odd wild elephant on the rampage, but no Cornish bulls as far as we know." Jon muttered a happy and hopeful response to this gem of trekking philosophy.

We continued along the safety of the hedge until the bulls had been left quite a way behind. Our direction of travel was still basically in the direction of Pendeen village, but without a path to guide us, we were just guessing about a viable way to get out of this field system and the 'shortcut' it promised us at the start of our detour.

Persistence paid off, and we eventually toiled our way back to the lane that led us straight into Pendeen village. We found the bus stop for St Just, and with about ten minutes to wait before the bus was scheduled to arrive, we went into a very convenient convenience store just opposite the bus stop. Stocking up on snacks for the following day's journey didn't take us long, and the bus arrived right on time. I knew that Jon had put in a brave but exhausting effort that day because when I used my bus pass to get my usual free ride, he barely noticed; there weren't any indignant comments, and that really was worrying. It was at this point that I began to consider seriously the possibility of Jon's injury making it inadvisable for him to take on the trip to Africa and the trek up Kilimanjaro. Would I go by myself if the worst came to the worst? I didn't relish the prospect, but not going would lead to the loss of a lot of money. Jon's insurance would cover him if his doctor confirmed that he was unfit to travel, but I wouldn't have that option. Oh well, time would tell.

The bus dropped us off in the centre of St Just, and we soon found our way to the hostel. Jon was very weary by this time, but he could still walk fairly well. We soon registered at the reception desk and found our private room with the usual two bunks. By the time we sorted out the gear for the morning, had a shower, and had a rest in the lounge, the evening meal was being served. The meal was welcome as we hadn't eaten anything substantial since breakfast in St Ives that morning.

Jon bought a round of drinks for us to take back out to the lounge, so I knew that he just wasn't his usual self. I didn't make any comment about this as it might have put him off buying me another drink at some distant time in the future.

I opened the topic of whether or not he would be fit enough to tackle the hard, final day's training walk lined up for the following day. It seemed that it was fifty-fifty at this stage of the game, and we would need to wait until the morning to see how he felt about the injury.

* * *

Sleep was no problem at all that night, although I did have a dim recollection of dreaming about chasing two recalcitrant bulls around a certain field until I exhausted them to a standstill. Jon was a lot brighter this morning, but his leg had not improved enough to attempt the long and demanding route to Penzance, especially as even with full fitness it would need a brisk pace to get us to the town in time for the last train of the evening for Plymouth. That was it; decision made – we would take the bus to Penzance from St Just after having breakfast here at the hostel. We should be back in Plymouth by late morning, and Jon could rest that injury. There were seven weeks left before we would set off for Africa, so Jon could hopefully nurse the injury back to health and full strength again. In any event, we had finished the intensive training on that great walk from Minehead in Somerset to St Just in Cornwall; over two hundred and fifty miles of striking scenery, ever-changing and glorious skies, interesting meals, and many memorable people we had met on the journey. It wouldn't be long now before the next, and very different, adventure would be opening up for us. See you then.

EIGHTEEN

Jon had to travel back to his home in Twyford after resting for a few days in Plymouth at his mother's home. But, before he left, we managed to sort out a number of admin points for our fast-approaching journey to Africa.

Jon had researched the flight availability to Tanzania back in May and had done a good job of navigating the internet in what had seemed to me like a mini-labyrinth, but I must admit to being a 'dotty digital dinosaur'. He had found one flight that would involve a ten-hour wait for our connecting flight in the airport at Addis Ababa. Having spoken to some acquaintances who had used that route, they didn't speak at all favourably about their experience, and they only had a three-hour wait in the airport, let alone ten hours! And bearing in mind that we would then have another few hours to wait for the connecting flight from Nairobi to Kilimanjaro Airport, this was a non-starter for us.

Jon finally found that our best option was by British Airways 747 from Heathrow direct to Nairobi. There would then be a two- to three-hour wait for our connecting flight to Kilimanjaro Airport. This wasn't the cheapest option, but it was worth the extra hundred or so pounds to avoid the long connection delays on the other viable routes on the outwards and return journeys. So,

British Airways it would be. We booked the flight back in June, so there was no problem at this point in time with only seven weeks to go before the start of our journey. The other favourable thing with this flight plan was that we would fly on Saturday the 8th of September and be in the hotel at Arusha late that same day. We would then have the Sunday to fully recover from the long flight before starting out on the trek on the Monday morning.

With the flight bookings taken care of, we could now start to organise the outstanding requirements that would need to be in place before we set off in seven weeks. Jon's application for his visa had already been forwarded to the Tanzanian Embassy in London. Our trek organiser recommended that we should apply six or seven weeks before the date of departure, so I put my application together, with the help of the embassy's website, and sent it off.

Another thing to arrange was a visit to the doctor to discuss the medical requirements for that part of Africa. A yellow fever jab was strongly recommended, as were the different possible medications to ward off malaria, but everything else seemed to be all right on my medical record. The yellow fever jab would be carried out by our local pharmacy chain, and the options for malaria protection would also be dealt with by them. I arranged an appointment for the following week, so that was another thing well in hand. It is surprising just how many threads need to be drawn together for a trip like ours.

The need for a yellow fever jab was, surprisingly, not purely for medical reasons. Even if your doctor didn't think that you would need one from a strictly medical point of view, there is always the chance that an official at the Kilimanjaro Airport would insist on seeing your proof that you had received the jab for yellow fever. This is purportedly because you had spent time in Nairobi, albeit just in the airport terminal. It is not unknown that in the absence of proof that you had received the jab, you could still tip the official to be waved through as the easy option. These stories are documented, but as far as I know, unproven at this time.

Jon was on his way back to the family, and I had a week to wait before the jab and the assessment for the type of malaria treatment I would need. It now seemed like a good opportunity to think back over our three multi-day training walks in order to learn any lessons for the African trek up the mountain. It was also a good opportunity to start working through the packing list provided by the expedition company to see if I needed to buy any extra gear. Equally as important was the need to order up some more American dollars, as this was the preferred currency in the part of Tanzania we were going to.

I thought back over our training so far, and the first thing to strike me was that, with the exception of one or two minor disagreements, we walked well together, and any disagreements were quickly nullified, especially if Jon came round amicably to my way of thinking! We shared a lively sense of humour, and Jon tolerated my wicked sense of humour at his expense with the grace and good nature of a real, but long-suffering, friend.

Jon's various past injuries still had an effect on him, but he was stoical about this. He hit a strong and steady uphill pace and maintained this until he reached the top of the hill or cliff path, no matter what. My pace was more comfortable at a steady, but a little slower, pace than Jon's. I would sometimes take a short breather break or two on the steepest and longest climbs, but basically, I did not slow Jon down too much.

My breathing on the more demanding ascents was better than I could have hoped for. Whether this was a good indicator of the way I would tolerate the often-crushing effects of Kilimanjaro's high altitude remained to be seen.

I didn't suffer any stiffness or joint pains throughout our training walks. This was almost certainly due to my training in the local gym and to the excellent advice I received from the gym instructors.

Jon's only apparent problem was with his aggravated Achilles tendon injury. This was clearly painful at times, but Jon has a high pain tolerance.

Being a natural leader, Jon was nevertheless willing to be led where my knowledge of the terrain and experience of backpacking in general were helpful. I listened to Jon to get his ideas about all aspects of our training, route-planning, and general welfare on the trail; it was a successful working relationship. All of this pointed to a continuing amity for when we trekked up the mountain together in six weeks' time.

Several weeks before, I had ordered the main amount of the dollars I guessed that I would need. The exchange rate happened to be extremely favourable at that time, so it made sense to arrange this early. But in the notes that came with our packing list, it was mentioned that dollars in small denominations were useful for tipping and small-value purchases. The main holding of dollars I had received earlier only had ten dollar notes as the smallest denomination, so I ordered another two hundred dollars in denominations of one dollar and five dollars. Jon did the same, and this proved to be an ideal mix of notes throughout the trip when combined with some of the larger denominations. The good news was that, because most of the time was spent on the mountain and on safari, I spent far less than I anticipated.

With all that area of the admin sorted out, it was time to work through the comprehensive packing list. The list from the trip organiser was clearly based on a lot of experience, and I worked through it methodically and slowly to make sure that nothing was overlooked.

The first item on the list was a mountain jacket. Bearing in mind how cold it could become on or near the summit of the mountain at up to 5895 metres, a good-quality down or synthetic-filled garment that would give excellent protection at that height had to be a top priority. Jon had already bought a Rab Electron jacket, and I added an identical jacket to my 'to buy' list. Jon had tried his out on a cold winter's day in the UK, and he found it a little too warm, even though he was wearing it at a rugby match as a relatively static spectator, with other spectators around him shivering in their normally adequate winter clothing.

Trousers were recommended in three forms. Lined thermal trousers for the summit ascent, lighter weight trousers for the majority of the trek, and shorts could be a good idea for sunny and warm days in the earlier part of the trek to the summit camp in the higher altitudes.

Layering would be absolutely necessary when the temperature dropped as we climbed higher. In essence, this would consist of a thermal base layer or warm material inner layer. The modern materials that wick away moisture and dry quickly are ideal for a base layer, and it is certainly recommended to take along long johns and a long-sleeved top for the night ascent to the summit. The mid-layer acts as the first barrier to retain a lot of the warmth radiating out from the base layer. This layer could consist of a lightweight fleece or a custom-made mid-layer designed for just this job. Top layers come in various types, and they also help to retain the warmth around the wearer's body. This layer could be a heavier fleece, a mountain jacket, a substantial softshell jacket, or something similar to achieve a comparable result. In wet weather, or cold and windy conditions, a tough waterproof and breathable anorak will complete the layering around the main part of the body. But the fact that the top garments are going to be worn over the other layers will probably mean that this outer clothing should be a size larger than usual in order to fit well.

The hands also come in for warming attention. Gloves offer a wide range of choice, depending on what conditions the wearer could be confronted with on a particular expedition. Our route on Kilimanjaro involves a scramble up the Barranco Wall on the fourth day of the trek. Some accounts I have read about this scramble paint an off-putting picture of the ascent. Again, mention of danger lurking at every footstep presents a frightening prospect. Descriptions of the precipitous falls awaiting the careless or the plain unlucky may make one alarmed at the thought of a one-way ticket on this trip. But other accounts of 'the wall' do not present anything like as bleak a picture of the scramble up the Barranco;

time will tell. The ideal gloves for this section of the climb up the mountain are the gloves that can keep your hands warm while at the same time give you a surfacing on the palms that are specially designed for scrambling on rocks.

Higher up the mountain, when the much colder conditions often kick in, thicker gloves with great warming qualities come into their own. I talked with an experienced climber about this, and his verdict was that the outer gloves should be of a generous size to allow liner gloves to be worn comfortably. The liner gloves that seem to be first-class for these conditions are the ones made from silk. This is the glove combination I finally decided on, and it worked really well. One final point about the outer gloves is that, where possible, opt for the waterproof and breathable version. These chunky sub-zero gloves will probably be over the top at lower altitudes, so a suitable pair of waterproof and breathable gloves of medium weight would be a good thing to pack as well where the weather calls for gloves.

A muff is also a great item to take with you. These come into their own whenever the conditions become dry and dusty. It seems that conditions like those often prevail on the way down from the summit when trekkers are invited to scree-run rapidly down from the heights that were so painfully climbed the night before. But even with a muff to block the dust from getting into your throat from the other scree-runners in front of you, it would be wise to leave a good, safe distance.

Boots of the right type and quality are obviously important for a trip like this. They should be robust and comfortable, well broken in, and with plenty of life left in them. Another thing to consider is that you can lace them comfortably over a pair of good-quality trekking socks and ideally with a pair of liner socks being worn as well. The aim is to prevent your feet sliding enough inside the boots in a way that lets your toes bang into the inside of the toe caps, especially going downhill for any length of time. Spare laces are also highly recommended for carrying in the daypack just in case.

Gaiters are also a good item of gear to have with you. These are particularly useful when trudging over broken ground where tiny fragments of stone or sand could work their way over the tops of the boots, down into the boot's interior, and start to cause irritations and abrasions to your feet. Gaiters also come into their own on muddy terrain.

A woollen hat that is warm and can be pulled down over the ears when necessary is another item that I would class as vital on the type of trip we are going on. Hats of this kind are also excellent for holding the hood from an anorak in just the right position for visibility, and they also make a hood more comfortable. And bearing in mind that ten per cent or more of body heat can be lost through the top of the head, I always carry a spare to be on the safe side in case one hat gets lost or blown away. A warm scarf is also a great piece of clothing to take along. This will make it cosier when the cold wind is battering you and stop rain from working its way into the opening of the hood and down onto your inner clothing.

For Kilimanjaro, snow goggles are highly recommended for coping with the glare from the sun and glaciers on the summit. Sun lotion of factor thirty plus and lip cream are also a great idea, and not only for the summit. The sun can cause burning even on the lower slopes of the mountain.

Walking poles are another excellent idea for the climb. They will help with the ascents, especially if they are shortened to suit the angle at which you are climbing. The poles also often make the downwards slopes easier to negotiate. In this case, the poles will ideally be lengthened to suit the angle of descent. However, the nature of the ground must be taken into account. There will be some ground conditions where it will make more sense to have both hands free, for example where there are boulders tumbled and jumbled for you to negotiate, or other types of potentially dangerous terrain where a rapid response would be needed if you slipped.

Water-carrying facilities are another vital aspect on the packing list. Hydration systems have become popular in recent years, and I must admit that over the training walks I did with Jon, the concept really started to become a big feature with me. The notes about our trip emphasised that as we trekked higher up the mountain, the more we should drink to help to minimise the effects of altitude. Four or more litres a day should be our goal as we started to feel the altitude effect. That is a lot of water to drink in one day, and it is also a lot to keep waking one up through the night!

Water bottles should also be taken. They are particularly useful on the cold night ascent to the summit. It is usual for the supply pipe connected to a hydration system to freeze solid on the way to the summit, hence the need for a water bottle that can be carried in a pocket inside the outer clothing to keep the water in a drinkable form. Several accounts I read about that summit night by other climbers described how they had to force themselves to drink, or even to eat, anything to keep their strength up. That night ascent seemed like a sub-zero nightmare. I wonder how Jon and I will cope with it.

I may have mentioned earlier that our support team would carry the tents, cooking gear, food, water, our sleeping bags, sleeping pads, and everything that we trekkers won't be carrying in our daypacks. The daypacks are recommended to be about thirty litres carrying capacity, so we will not be overburdened for climbing up into unfamiliar altitudes with diminishing oxygen in the air. Rain covers for the packs are strongly recommended, although when we ascend the mountain in September, rainfall is usually much less than in other months of the year, with the exception of October.

The type of sleeping bag needs careful consideration in view of the low temperatures we can expect at night. Minus fifteen degrees Celsius may be anticipated on Kilimanjaro on particularly cold nights, but it can dip occasionally below that point. I invested in a sleeping bag to meet that specification, and I also bought a liner that could keep the ambient temperature comfortable even when the temperature dropped to several points below that. The trick is to find a sleeping bag that can meet the requirements without being too heavy. I have an Antarctic-quality sleeping bag that could easily do the job, but at 2.5 kilograms, it is certainly too heavy for backpacking, but it may be useful at home during an exceptionally cold winter or maybe in a mini Ice Age!

A useful addition to the sleeping bag and liner is a pair of great-quality bed socks. I have a pair of these with the inside surface made up of brushed wool. These socks are invaluable when cold feet could make it difficult to sleep.

I always found that a satisfactory pillow suitable for backpacking was difficult to find. Finally, the penny dropped, and I now take along a pillowcase that can be used to hold layers of folded clothing. That clothing has to be taken on the trip in any event, so it is no problem. My mattress is a simple piece of foam about three centimetres thick and cut to cover the area from my neck to the base of my spine. This is placed over my thinner, closed-cell mat for good insulation. I also cut the foam as narrow as I can get away with in order to keep the carrying weight to a minimum. A good alternative to this if you are an advanced yoga practitioner is to sleep in a state of levitation to avoid the effects of the rough ground (!).

Illumination is also highly important after dark both inside and outside the tent. The night ascent of Kilimanjaro definitely demands a head torch and probably a backup hand torch, with standby batteries for both. A tent light that can be suspended from the roof of the inner tent is also a big help for finding things in the tent and for reading by.

Another great piece of equipment to have with you is a collapsible 'pee' bottle to get around the problem of trying to find a suitable toilet spot at some distance from the tent at night. It seems that they can be bought these days for women and men, and they are worth every penny you spend.

Naturally, spare clothing needs to be packed, but I wouldn't be too diligent about packing a lot. There wouldn't be opportunities for showering, or even a proper washdown on this trip, so changes of clothing would not be a top priority until the return to base in the hotel in Arusha where our clean clothing would be stored. It would be amazing to get under a well-earned shower after six days of hard climbing and minimal washing. But all would not be lost, as I quickly learned while backpacking in the UK that body wipes, or baby wipes, can act as a portable 'shower'.

First aid items are also important to pack for the trip. Medication for headaches, indigestion, and constipation, or its opposite, are one of the first concerns. I usually pack something like E45 anti-itching cream, a wound-healing gel, and an antiseptic gel. Plasters, bandages, wound dressings are also part of my first aid kit, even though on this trip the team would probably have all of those things in the main first aid pack. I always pack a pair of folding scissors and a pair of tweezers in case I pick up a thorn or splinter.

Everyone must take their own toilet paper on the trip, as well as toilet gear and towel(s). I also pack a small number of miniature clothes pegs and a lightweight washing line. This is useful not only for any washing that may be convenient to do but also for drying out any clothing that has become wet through rain or just perspiration.

Other items will probably include snacks and treats in quantities enough for oneself and (if you want to be really popular) for your porters as well. I decided to follow the advice of the trip organisers and take throat and cough sweets. It seems that these can be helpful if your breathing becomes laboured or even congested at those higher altitudes. One of the packs of throat sweets I took along was the famous Fisherman's Friend lozenges. These are particularly strong, and I will tell you later what happened when I offered these lozenges around to some of our porters.

Personal items such as a device to play favourite music or audio books can be a great comfort through the long watches of the night when sleep is elusive or on long treks during the day. A lightweight camera is always good to take, as is a small favourite book, a notebook, and a pen or pencil. Also, the passport with the visa for Tanzania, vaccination record, money, and the notes and itinerary provided for the trip, which also include important telephone numbers to use in case of difficulties. And that seems to be about it.

***

Jon came back again during the following week, and we went into the main pharmacy in the city to get our yellow fever jabs. It didn't hurt until the following day, and even then, it was only a minor ache. But while we were in the pharmacy, we made enquiries about the most appropriate type of anti-malaria tablets to use in Tanzania. Jon made a note of the recommended type and ordered them online from a reputable supplier. The tablets we ordered needed to be taken for about a week before the trip, during the time spent in Africa, and for another three weeks after our return to the UK; quite a task, but worth it to avoid malaria.

It was just after having the jab that I realised that there hadn't been a response from the Tanzanian Embassy with my visa. I decided to wait a few more days to see if it arrived. Time passed, and there still wasn't anything from the visa department. It was time to give them a call to find out if there was a problem with my application.

I was on the point of telephoning the embassy later that morning when something unfortunate happened. My wife, Judith, had picked up two calls that morning from a foreign-sounding caller who wanted our bank details in order to arrange a refund for us because of an overcharge on one of our accounts of several hundred pounds. Yes! You guessed it; it was a crude attempt at a scam.

Shortly after the second call came in, a third call came through from another foreign-sounding voice. Judith told the caller in no uncertain terms to get off our line and take a long walk off a short pier (although she didn't phrase it as politely as in my version).

She was still smirking about the neat way she had dealt with that third call when the telephone rang yet again. I answered the call this time and found myself talking with a gentleman from the Tanzanian Embassy who was calling about my delayed visa. But within a few short moments, he complained bitterly to me about having just received a very abusive response on our line when he called just a minute or so ago, and not only that, but the lady who had answered him slammed the receiver down on his call.

I apologised abjectly for Judith's response and tried to explain what had led up to her uncharacteristic response. The gentleman was still shocked and deeply indignant at the way he had been spoken to, and I assured him that I would talk to Judith about the offence that had been caused. This started to pacify our caller, and he then went on to tell me why he was calling. This was the problem: I had sent in my visa request using the wrong method of payment, and I would need to resend the application with a cheque as quickly as possible in order to receive the visa in time for the flight to Tanzania. But he thought that an online application would be far better at this stage. I had in fact followed the instructions on the embassy website about the different ways to pay, but it later became clear that this was an older method of payment that had been withdrawn. It didn't seem like a good idea at this stage to argue the point with him in view of the indignity he had suffered when he called us, but when I checked the website again, the older method of payment was still shown even though I had taken a contorted route to find it in the masses of pages on the site.

I apologised again for the unfortunate mix-up when Judith answered his call, and I think we were forgiven. We only had about two weeks left before the flight, so I fervently hoped that he wouldn't hold any grudges and delay the visa until the very last minute to make me sweat. In the event, I received the visa six days before my departure, so 'all's well that ends well'. I tried to make it clear to Judith just how much grief her verbal assault had caused, but we just had to laugh about the way fate had tricked us that morning.

The final part of the admin for this trip was my travel insurance. This had been arranged earlier in the year, but, for my peace of mind, I needed to double check that I was adequately covered for the trip ahead.

Travel insurance that covered the cost of a possible rescue or evacuation and medical expenses in full, together with the cost of a possible repatriation to the UK was compulsory. I had submitted a copy of the insurance policy to our trip organiser, and this was deemed to be comprehensive enough.

The type of insurance we needed in order to be covered above two thousand metres was a special travel policy, and because I was seventy-five, this raised the cost of the cover. But in the event, the price of £181 seemed reasonable in view of the extra risk that I might need to be evacuated if the going was just too tough for me. Evacuation could be a tricky thing because it all depended upon the judgement of the trek leader. If I was slowing the group down too much, or if the leader considered that my health or fitness just wasn't up to the climb, then I would be evacuated without any scope for appeal. The other possibility could be that an ankle or knee injury on the mountain might be a more serious problem for me than for a younger person. This again might lead to an evacuation that the insurer would have to pay for. And all of this was in addition to the constant threat of the altitude effect that could creep up on climbers of any age and frequently did within many groups. In spite of all these possibilities, I remained upbeat and couldn't wait for the remaining week to pass before starting the journey that I had been training so hard for over the past months. Jon had already travelled back to his home in Twyford, and the plan was for me to drive up to his place on the 7th of September, stay overnight, and set off very early the following day for Heathrow Airport by the local railway service. We needed to be at the airport by 7.15am, and we were lucky enough to be able to travel on one of the first trains in the morning from Jon's local station.

So, everything was set fair at long last for our outwards journey; a journey of 4242 miles to Nairobi Airport, then a local flight of 145 miles to Kilimanjaro Airport. That would be a total journey time of nine hours thirty-five minutes if everything ran to schedule.

The last few days dragged without mercy, but the 7th of September eventually arrived. I said my farewells to Judith, drove out of the driveway, and the adventure had actually started. Africa here we come!

ND
NINETEEN

Jon and I arrived at Heathrow on the Saturday morning within the recommended time frame of three hours before our flight was due to take off. Jon had been a police sergeant here at the airport back in his early twenties, so he knew his way around the place with the confidence of an expert navigator. We negotiated the registration phase, the luggage check-in, and security checks at dizzying speed, and it wasn't even 8.15am. Our flight was scheduled to leave at 10.25am, so a leisurely breakfast in one of the departure restaurants beckoned.

The flight left on time, and the British Airways 747 sped us to Nairobi on quite a pleasant trip. There was a two-hour wait in Nairobi Airport for our connecting flight to Kilimanjaro Airport on a small turbojet plane. The difference between that aircraft and the 747 was immense, but after an hour's flight, we arrived safely at our destination. We had made it to Tanzania, and our transport was waiting outside the airport to whisk us away through the night to the hotel at Arusha, which is about a forty-five-minute drive on a pretty good road. It was a quiet road at that time of day and so dark that we didn't see much of the countryside.

It was approaching midnight by the time we reached the hotel, but there was a most welcome meal arranged for us after we had been shown our room and dropped off our gear. We both slept well that night, and from all accounts, I didn't snore, which Jon treated as an unexpected bonus. I think he had a short memory of his experiences in the hostel dormitories where we reportedly had chronic snorers to the left and to the right of us on each of the nights that we slept in one of these strange environments. All my more refined snoring couldn't compare with that experience for Jon. We awoke at about 8am and, after washing, went down to the dining room for breakfast and to meet our trek leader.

Not all the food at breakfast was recognisable, but it tasted all right whatever it was. Patrick, our English trek leader, spotted us as soon as he entered the fairly busy dining room. He was a retired officer from an army regiment, quite short, and with an engaging manner. After explaining various things about the trek ahead of us, he confirmed that three other trekkers would be joining us later that day from the UK: two young ladies and a young man. It seems that all three were in their early thirties, so even Jon at forty-eight would be relatively elderly on this trip, and at seventy-five, I would be way over the hill. I must admit to some last-minute doubts creeping into my mind about the wisdom of being here at this time of life. At all events, I was here now and would just have to get stuck in and do my best. At least we had done a lot of good training for the challenges ahead.

Patrick told us about some of his experiences as a trekking guide in different countries, but Kilimanjaro had been new to him until the previous week when he went up with a group for the first time. I should explain at this stage that our group was to be led by a very experienced local guide, and there would also be an assistant guide. In addition, there would be twenty-one other members of the team, and these would consist of porters, cooks, and general assistants. Patrick would be there as a liaison man and to generally look out for the interests of the five of us from the UK. Swahili isn't an easy language, so Patrick would also be the conveyor of information and instructions from the group high command. We would be starting the trip on the following day once our group was fully assembled, so the whole trip would span from Monday to the following Saturday.

With breakfast finished, it was time for Patrick to check our gear to make sure that we had all the essentials and that they were up to the required standard. It was a bit like a kit muster in the armed forces, but it made a lot of sense to carry out a thorough check of everything that we should have, as directed on the packing list provided by the tour company.

Patrick was happy with the gear we had brought with us and particularly liked our Rab Electron mountain jackets and Scarpa boots. Jon hadn't packed his head torch, so Patrick arranged for one to be brought along on the following day from the supply of hire equipment held locally. So far, so good – everything appeared to be in place for the departure early on the following morning. We decided to just relax in the hotel for the day and have lunch and dinner in the hotel later on. The city of Arusha is a bit of a mixed bag, and the area we were in didn't have many Europeans walking around the small shanty-type shops or around the busy streets. There were locals of certain types who would try to exploit visitors in the city if they had half a chance – a little like London in that respect – so we decided to just stay in the hotel and chill out until the other three arrived later in the day.

We chatted to Patrick for most of the morning and then went to the dining room for an excellent lunch. The afternoon was spent relaxing and catching up on our sleep before the rigors of the expedition would undoubtedly make strenuous demands on us.

It wasn't until mid-evening that James, the first of our other three trekkers, arrived. We were just going into dinner, but James was so travel-weary that he just wanted to sort out his gear for the morning and grab a few hours' sleep. The two young ladies arrived late that night, and we didn't meet them until the following morning at our early breakfast. All three of the new arrivals were easy to get along with, and that was a real bonus after reading about the interrelational problems that can sometimes crop up on expeditions. The two young ladies had known each other for several years and had planned for some time to come on this trip together. James was a sporty and fit guy, and the women also were into fitness, running, and biking. It confirmed to me when I heard this that our training effort was time well spent.

All five of us were ready to leave by the departure time of 9am the following morning, and special arrangements had been made on our behalf with the hotel for a storeroom to be put at our disposal where we could leave the luggage that would not be needed on the mountain for safekeeping. This was particularly useful for Jon and me because we were going on a three-day safari the day after our return from Kilimanjaro, so we had various clothing and gear that needed to be stored.

The two local group leaders came into the hotel to meet us, and I felt immediately confident that we were in good hands. David was our local Tanzanian chief guide, and he had climbed Kilimanjaro about two hundred times in various weather conditions and temperatures during the changes encountered over the typical twelve-month annual cycle. It was now time to load up the expedition transport outside the hotel and meet many of our support team before setting off on the way to the mountain which was about a two-hour drive away.

The guys in the support team were buzzing around the vehicle loading our gear into the racks on the roof. They were happy and apparently as enthusiastic as we were to get started. Their lives, on average, are financially tenuous with a big reliance on trips to Kilimanjaro and Mount Meru for their incomes. Payment is regulated but fairly modest for the hard work they do; having said that, these are sought-after jobs in the local economy. It was becoming clear that the bonuses we were asked to pay formed an important part of their income, and I could see in even the first few minutes that they would earn every penny of the recommended bonuses to be paid on the final day as we were just approaching the end of our journey.

The gear had been loaded to the satisfaction of the chief guide, and off we drove through the interesting streets and marketplaces of Arusha. One of the striking things we saw on the pavements was the number of people walking along carrying great bunches of bananas over their shoulders. It seems that bananas are an important part of the diet in this part of the world. I must say that the local people look fit and healthy on the food they eat. They are full of energy and have a generally buoyant spirit. As we gradually got to know the guys in our support team, the more I came to admire them. They called me 'Babu', which apparently means wise elder or grandfather. Jon, being a creative soul, lengthened this to 'baboon'; need I say more?!

Our two vehicles motored on along the fairly busy road towards Kilimanjaro. There were many little townships and villages along our route, and these were all bustling and vibrant. Many narrow tracks branched away from the road into the flat terrain, and these often led to what appeared to be small farming areas. All of this was acting out under the huge dome of the hazy blue sky. We hadn't yet reached a point where we could get our first view of Kilimanjaro, but the general excitement was growing in our vehicle, even among the members of the support team, many of whom had climbed this mountain numerous times. If it has that strength of attraction on these guys, it really must be an exceptional place.

The mountain appeared after we had travelled for about two hours along the road. It was huge, even from quite a distance away. As we gradually moved closer to the mountain, its dominance became unmistakeable. It was the most awesome geological spectacle I had ever seen. It reached up into the pure blue sky out of the flat terrain all around it in the most dramatic and surprising way you could imagine. How could its giant presence just appear out of nowhere like that? Television programmes show us geological marvels of the world, but the impact upon the senses in real life are enormous. I wish my word power could do it justice, but even then, you would have to see it yourself to experience its sheer visual and emotional power. I will never forget that first impression of the mountain, the biggest free-standing volcano on the world's landmass. A hallow of clouds encircled the mountain about two thirds of the way up, but the summit was still visible. I shuddered as the image of the long and daunting climb up there gradually formed in my mind. We wanted an exciting trek, and we had chosen a monster. I just hoped that this mountain didn't choose anyone in our group to be one of its occasional victims.

After a few more miles down this fascinating road, we turned off into a minor road that wound its way up through banana plantations and what appeared to be coffee crops and nut crops as well. Tiny farms were scattered along the gradually ascending road, and the not-unpleasant smells of farm animals, rich soil, and crops all around us filtered into the vehicle as we moved up through the foothills.

Then, all of a sudden, we were at Machame Gate, the assembly and departure point for the various groups like ourselves who would be spending the next six days trekking closer to heaven than many of us had ever been before: 5895 metres, 19,340 feet, about two thirds of the height of Mount Everest.

There were plenty of other groups in the open-air assembly area, and the excitement could be felt immediately upon entering. What first seemed like a Temple of Babel was a mixture of different languages from countries around the world. Climbing this mountain is justifiably popular.

There were small shops and stalls scattered around the area, so things like maps and guides of Kilimanjaro could be readily bought and at reasonable prices. Jon bought a striking sun hat with a sensible brim to shield his eyes in the strong sunlight. I brought my favourite sun hat along, and this was bought several years before in Provence, France.

Various admin steps had to be attended to before we could set off up the mountain. Passport checks, paperwork from our tour company, names, addresses, and next-of-kin all had to be registered and verified against their records at the office. I think that this was partly because the park fee for climbing this mountain is not cheap, and although this had been paid as part of our overall trip charge, the authorities wanted to be sure that everyone on their list for that day's departure could be sanctioned.

One thing that came out of this check was that David, our trek leader, found out that on this Machame route, the oldest person to climb the mountain was about seventy, but it wasn't clear whether he made it to the summit. At seventy-five, I could be the oldest person on record to climb this monster on this particular route, assuming that I made it to the top!

There were sheltered sitting areas provided around the assembly area, and our team members invited us over to one of these while we waited for all the checks to be completed. To our surprise, in came two of the lads carrying large cardboard boxes. It soon became obvious that these contained our packed lunches, so in we dived before the rush started. Jon's tapeworm was alive and kicking, but what it would think of the food in store for us on the mountain was open to speculation.

We enjoyed the packed lunch sitting in the cooling shade of the waiting area, and it wasn't long before everyone was 'admined' and we eventually got under way. Here we were at long last at the start of what was to become a remarkable six days.

TWENTY

The first steps on the upwards journey to the summit were on a well-surfaced road leading into the start of the rainforest. It was about midday, and the sun's heat rippled down with legendary African strength. It wasn't long before the road ran out, and the forest track began. I could see clearly why some of the other expeditions I had read about made a point concerning the tree roots threading their slippery way across the track. Today was dry, but in wet weather, walking on the tree roots would need caution.

Being in the forest was more comfortable for walking. The direct heat had been more contained by the thicker forestation, and the glare from the sun's light had been reduced considerably. The sunlight itself was stencilling through the animated tree canopy and scribbling dappled patterns along the cool pathway. The upwards slope wasn't too steep at first, but that gradually changed as we ascended. This rainforest was regarded as the first of the five main zones we would trek through on our way up the mountain. Rich volcanic soil and copious amounts of rainfall clearly nourished these thick concentrations of forest, and it wasn't long before its wildlife started to appear close to the pathway:

Our group trekking up into the Kilimanjaro rainforest on the start of our journey

Colobus monkeys were the first on the scene. They are shy creatures, with striking white manes draping over their black fur. Their agility is wonderful to watch as they leap fearlessly from tree to tree. One of them showed a distinct fascination with Jon. We didn't spot any of the so-called blue monkeys, which are actually black and charcoal grey, but it seems that they are in this forest in fair numbers.

Snakes are reputed to live in the thicker forest areas, but the guys in the support team have never encountered one here on the path so far. There were bird calls from time to time, and although it is difficult to see, the silver-cheeked hornbill with its donkey-like bray of a call is a feature of this forest. It seems that the turaco bird is also seen occasionally here in the forest and can be identified by a flash of crimson on its wings. How different all this seemed from our birds on Cornwall's coast path! I must say that I already very much missed the seagulls soaring with the thermals over and around our sea cliffs, but there were plenty of interesting things going on here to compensate.

The trail we were on would take us to our first camp at 2980 metres where it seems that our support team would have the tents set up for us, tea and coffee ready just as we arrived, and the smell of a welcome meal being prepared coming from the dining tent. This first short day of trekking covered eighteen kilometres of gradually steepening ascent, and we entered the camp just as it got dark. We all had our headlamps ready just in case we were delayed.

Considering that the weather we had been walking through had been pleasantly warm, I think most of us felt quite stretched by the climb. My thoughts went back to the accounts I had read about this same route in wet and chilly weather. Some of those trekkers felt so all-in by the time they reached the first camp that all they wanted to do was to get out of their wet gear and sleep. One or two felt so weary that they had serious doubts about even attempting the second day of trekking, so it must have been really bad for them on the first day of their expedition.

Our group, being there in a much drier time of the year, were doing all right so far. Having said that, that time of year can be a lot colder, especially at night, so we all had our fingers crossed for nothing too extreme.

Just as I was thinking about all these things, the campsite loomed up out of the semi-darkness just as the earliest stars were sparkling their way onto the vast stage of the night sky above this mountain with its clear atmosphere. We were now about three thousand metres, 9750 feet above sea level, and I didn't yet feel any effects from the altitude, even though I had never climbed above 1200 metres before.

The aroma of our evening meal being prepared was so inviting that I couldn't help myself, I just had to pay a visit to the lads in the kitchen section of the dining tent to say hello and to ask about the meal they had lined up for us. They seemed to love the idea that 'Babu' took time out after a demanding first day of trekking to visit them. The language difficulties were soon resolved, and it was established that our meal was to be a hearty soup, some sort of meat (don't ask!), vegetables, pasta, and some type of savoury pancake. Dessert was a type of fruit pudding with something like custard, with sweet pancakes also available. Pancakes were a great favourite with our cooks, as subsequent days would confirm at evening meals and breakfast time.

I found our tent just as night descended in all its black mystery. The stars were populating the great dome of the heavens by this time, and the starlight intruded into the blackness with a timeless beauty. I learned as we experienced nights higher up the mountain that this stellar pageant was going to become increasingly awesome and affecting.

Jon had settled in well by this time, but when I asked him whether he had taken to camping yet, I had to duck as a bunched pair of sweaty trekking socks whizzed over my head. We had a fair amount of space in our Vango tent, and with our two sleeping bags laid out, there was enough room for our packs and other gear to be lined up between us down the middle of the groundsheet. There was the usual flysheet covering the inner tent, and the space offered between the two provided enough storage for boots and packs if we wanted to create more space inside the tent. The tent itself had double-zip doorways on both sides, and this was really convenient if we needed to get out of the tent during the night.

The evening had started to get decidedly colder, but our mountain jackets were not needed at this point; the softshell jackets, together with the layering provided by the inner wicking long-sleeved T-shirts and the mid-layer wicking garment did the business for this first evening.

We sorted out the gear for the next day, tidied the tent as far as we could, and then took a short rest before the call for the evening meal. The darkness had closed in around the camp by this time, and our head torches were needed even to get us to the nearby dining tent without tripping over guy ropes and pegs.

A large, hissing paraffin oil lamp did its best to light up the dining area, but the head torches, set at a low angle to avoid dazzling other people, were a real bonus. The five of us on the trip, together with Patrick our English guide, jammed into the cosy dining space, and impressions of the first day's trek came thick and fast. Everyone seemed to have enjoyed it, and there was a sense of excitement about the following day's trek up to the second camp on Shira Plateau. Shira was apparently a collapsed volcanic caldera and no longer posing any sort of problem, unlike Kibo at the top of the mountain which was merely sleeping and potentially dangerous.

Our chief guide, David, came in to see us just before the first course was served. He quickly talked us through the route for the following day and advised us to be prepared for a cold, but thankfully dry, night. The weather for the following day was forecast to be mainly sunny and partly hazy. He stressed the need to apply a high-factor sun lotion on exposed skin and to carry what we would need for the day in our daypacks, just as we had done this day. Patrick was lined up to record our physiological stats after the evening meal, and this would be a feature of every evening before the evening meal and mornings after breakfast. It was vital to keep everyone's health under review to ensure that we were not suffering from any worrying symptoms from the altitude or from the daily toll of climbing ever higher. Any developing problems had to be pinpointed as soon as possible so that effective action, or even an evacuation from the mountain, could be organised rapidly.

It was a jolly evening in the dining tent, and we got to know more about one another quite quickly through the life stories, goals, and big features of each one's life. The group was bonding into a cohesive, well-balanced whole, and everything pointed to a great, but demanding, week on this mountain.

We headed for the toilet on the edge of the campsite towards the end of the evening in an effort to try to prevent the need to leave the tent during the night to walk the hundred or so metres to the toilet hiding in the dense blackness right on the edge of the rainforest. Having already used these toilets, we knew what to expect. They were called long-drop toilets for obvious reasons. A hole in the wooden floor led to the catchment area about a yard beneath the flooring. There weren't any lights, so it was vitally important to take a torch or a headlamp, and this gave me an idea.

I was the last one to go into the toilet, and the other members of our group waited for me back on the track about twenty metres away. What a chance to really test Jon's friendship! I called out to him from the doorway of the toilet that I had accidently dropped my torch down the hole in the floor and into the long drop. Would he give me a hand to retrieve it, I asked? The answer to my friendship-testing question was a disappointing and very decisive no. The others laughed at this, but at least I knew the limits of Jon's proclaimed lifelong friendship. Had the situation been reversed, would I have dangled my arm down into the long drop to scrabble around for Jon's carelessly lost torch? Yes, of course I would (!!!).

Sleep came easily for me that first night, but Jon had only had his usual fitful spells of sleep. My secret weapon – the collapsible pee bottle – had to be used once during the night, and I congratulated myself on how it saved all the fuss and bother of having to attempt the tricky hike to the toilet. Unfortunately, this congratulation was misplaced.

Just after first light, one of the lads from the support team woke us up with steaming mugs of welcome tea and some biscuits. He also delivered a bowl of hot water and flannels for each of us to freshen up for the day ahead. What a great idea!

It was while I was getting the outer area of the tent organised that I found something that made me disbelieve what I was looking at. My pee bottle was safely secured at the top of the container, but I hadn't tightened the main threaded top of the bottle. Yes, the contents had leaked over the groundsheet just outside the inner door of the tent on my side, and a quantity had leaked into the floor area of the inner tent and right into the thin mattress under my sleeping bag. Knowing how hygiene-conscious Jon was, I stutteringly explained what had happened. His reaction couldn't possibly be described. All I can say is that it was so dramatic that our group leader, Patrick, came over to find out what had caused such an outpouring of indignation.

'Patrick the Peacemaker' quickly assessed the situation and suggested that I should put the mattress over the top of the dry tent so that the rising sun would sort it out while we were having breakfast. This worked well, and equilibrium was gradually restored as the morning progressed.

Breakfast was cheerful in the dining tent as we tucked into the pancakes, cooked breakfast, fruit, fruit juice, and coffee. Our medical readings were taken again to run a check against the previous evening's readings. Blood oxygen levels, heart rate, general questions about how we slept at this altitude, any trouble from headaches or tiredness, any aches or pains, and blood pressure. Surprisingly, a few headaches were reported, but I was all right so far. Jon's blood pressure was satisfactory, but if it had been taken during the discovery of the pee bottle malfunction episode, I shudder to think what it might have been. It could even have been high enough for him to be evacuated from the mountain as a precaution. He would never have spoken to me again had that been the case.

* * *

We had packed our gear for the day into the packs before breakfast. All the remaining gear had been packed into our kitbags ready for the porters to 'grab and go' as they wanted to be on the trail quickly in order to get to the next campsite and prepare everything for our arrival later in the day. Some of the remaining porters were helping to clear the dining tent and kitchen equipment. The tents, sleeping bags, and spare gear kitbags were being distributed and packed into manageable loads for the rest of the guys who were anxious to get moving up the mountain. We started out before these lads were able to leave, but it was truly amazing how they overtook us after about an hour. Considering the poor quality of the footwear and clothing that some of the porters were dressed in, and the big loads that they balanced on their heads or had strapped to their backs or both, it was a wonderful effort. Our admiration flowed out to them as they floated cheerfully past us with their jovial greetings of *jambo*; Swahili for hello.

As we got under way, I suddenly realised that Jon was speaking to me again and in his usual, friendly way. I should have been more careful with the collapsible bottle, and I certainly will be in future. It always takes me longer than average to reconcile myself to 'high tech'.

The path steepened as we ascended. Sunlight beamed in from the east and started to make it hot-going for us, even though our pace was being kept back by our experienced guide. Sun protector lotion of a high factor on exposed skin had been advised before we had left the campsite, and this, combined with sensible brimmed hats, was doing a great job in protecting us from this buoyant ball of nuclear fire bubbling away in the African sky. There were wispy, delicate shimmers of cloud floating around in cheeky defiance of the sun, but they didn't offer much in the way of occasional shade.

The terrain had changed dramatically. As soon as we had left the rainforest, zone two of the trek opened the door for us onto a landscape of fascinating plant life. This 'heather zone' was crammed with plants to send a biologist into ecstasy, especially over the giant senecios and the three-metre-high lobelias. But the heather gradually gave way to grassland with less in the way of abundant varieties of plant life.

This heather zone occupies a band from about 2,800 metres to 3,300 metres, which is approximately the height we were climbing to that day. We would be entering the Shira Plateau later in the day, and this was the area of the collapsed caldera of what had been a huge volcanic cone. The main volcanic cone, Kibo, which towered above Shira, had flung out giant tentacles of its lava that filled wide areas of this lower caldera, which was acting as a catchment area.

Adding even more to this adventure, a 1987 booklet I had read about Shira suggested that in some of the valleys of this general area, one could occasionally see buffalos, leopards, elands, and other animals, including the rare sighting of hunting lions. In the general absence of precautionary weaponry carried by any of our support group, or the trek leaders, I assumed that we were not in any imminent danger now that there were many more parties of trekkers on the mountain than when that booklet was written.

One of the other books I had read described the experiences of a group of family and friends trekking up this mountain during part of the rainy season in late December in order to reach the summit on New Year's Day. They were asked by their guide back at the meeting point in the hotel if two young ladies and their elderly father could be added to their party. This was agreed to by the original group members, and the enlarged group set off up the mountain on the Lemosho route which starts over to the west of where we joined the trail at Machame Gate. The two routes merge at the top of the Shira Plateau, about two and a half days into the trip.

Their first day was mercilessly wet for them as they were driven up through the first part of the forest, and because of their vehicles getting bogged down, the group had no choice but to walk some extra muddy and wearying miles to get to what should have been the starting point for the trek. This led to them not getting to their first camp until an appreciable time after darkness had fallen. They were drenched, dispirited, and so tired that at least one of their group was tempted to call it a day and ask to be evacuated the following morning. He was tired and aching all over, in spite of his months of training for the expedition. His wife sympathised with him, and he gradually decided to wait until the following morning before asking the group leader to arrange for his return to the hotel where they had started from. He knew how much his wife and children wanted to carry on regardless and how very much they wanted him to be part of the great adventure. Following a deeply uncomfortable first night in the tent, he bravely decided to carry on for another day. Walking wasn't too pleasant for him on that second day, but his mind was soon diverted by some shocking events.

It wasn't far into the morning's walk before one of the daughters with their father became angry with him. He was talking to a member of the group who had medical knowledge about some of the ailments that had come upon him since setting off on the trek from the day before. The father tried to ask what he was doing to upset his daughter, but this only served to fire up the human volcano into a seething and foul-mouthed rage. Everyone in the group was deeply shocked and offended that a daughter could talk to her father like that; everyone apart from the other daughter, that is, because she joined in with her sister in the affray.

No one wanted to create even more fuss for the group by launching into a counter-attack on the two devastatingly distracted daughters, so nothing was said at this point. But later that day, when the father asked if one of the group members could help him by passing him his water bottle from the back of his daypack, there was another furious outburst from the two daughters against the other members of the group, making it clear in the most colourful of language that they wanted nothing to do with the rest of the group at all.

Not only did this unnerve the whole group, but the group leader and those members of his team who had witnessed the scene were completely mystified as to what could have really been at the bottom of such a terrible outburst. As you can imagine, the rest of the trip needed to be handled with extreme diplomacy. The leader had taken over two hundred groups up this mountain, but nothing even remotely like this had ever happened before in his experience.

I reflected on our own good fortune in being with such a friendly and amiable group. I am sure that it is rare to have any trouble at all within the groups trekking up Kilimanjaro, but the expedition, whose story I have been relating, must be the stuff of nightmares for any of the guides who have heard about the shocking events surrounding that desperately unfortunate group aiming to reach the summit to celebrate New Year's Day on the roof of Africa.

Our own progress was going steadily, and Jon and I still hadn't felt any effects from the higher altitude, even though virtually every step was taking us higher. The fine weather helped us, in spite of the sun that blazed down in its cloud-free glory.

We came to a steeper section of the day's climb, and I noticed a slight difference in my breathing; it had become a little more laboured than I would have expected from such a slope. But just as I started to ponder on that, the assistant guide passed the word that it was nearly time for our packed lunch. This put new life into me, and I stopped worrying about Jon's tapeworm becoming increasingly frustrated deep in his hospitable intestinal tract.

Just at that moment, we saw a strange sight. On a flat rock a few metres off the track, a trekker from a group in front of us had got himself into a headstand with his inverted legs having allowed gravity to take them into something approaching the splits. It was a great effort, and our group applauded him, which sent his girlfriend into a fit of giggles. The things one sees when trekking up a mountain!

Our lunch stop was just beyond where the yoga demo had taken place. We sat in the sun and relished the welcome food that would give us the energy to complete the rest of the day's trek to the Shira campsite.

The afternoon passed by in a mixture of conversations with our new trekking companions, the group leader, and our tour guide, Patrick. I noticed that my breathing had returned to normal. *Cracked it!* I thought. My adjustment to the altitude had been rapid, or so I thought.

The second campsite came into view towards the end of the afternoon, and although it looked a lot more exposed than our previous camp, we were apparently above the rain zone. In fact, we were able to look down on what resembled the top of an ocean of continuous, sun-kissed cloud, much like being in an aircraft that had just flown up through the cloud from an overcast country into glorious sunshine.

Tea and cake were ready and waiting for us in the dining tent. These guys in the support team were certainly looking after us well. They still called me 'Babu' as a term of endearment (I think), and we all got on so well with them. Nothing was too much trouble for them, and you could just tell that they loved and appreciated this chance to give their families a regular income.

There was ample time to sort out our gear and clothing in the restricted space inside the tent, and before we knew it, we had the call for the evening meal. This was another happy get-together for our group, and although alcohol was not recommended at altitude, everyone seemed to be quite merry over the meal and coffee afterwards. I had the strong feeling that I was in with a chance to climb to the summit with this great group of fellow trekkers.

The darkness falls early in this part of the world, and we were tucked up in our sleeping bags by about 9pm. A gentle hum of other people talking in their tents lulled me to sleep, and even though I woke up occasionally during the night in order to change my position on the lumpy ground, I managed to get a fair night's sleep in preparation for the next day. That day would take us up to the Lava Tower and then down to Barranco Camp. The trek was going to be demanding, but at the end of it, we would be camping just across the valley from where the great rock barrier of the Barranco

Wall would look down on us with its notorious scrambling challenge that we were now committed to climb – whether we felt keen to attempt it or not – on the morning after.

* * *

"Washy, washy," said the voice outside our tent as full daylight was still wavering on whether to smile through the half-light or to have a lie-in. The hot water and flannels and steaming mugs of reviving tea were welcome. With sleepiness soon washed away, the smell of breakfast sizzling away over in the dining tent drove us to speed up our repacking of the surplus gear and clothing ready for the first wave of porters to pick up our kitbags and go. We could see from the steepness of the track forging ahead of us up the mountain that the porters, and the rest of us, were in for a tough day.

The sun's rays flooded down as a glorious morning sparkled into life. I turned to look down the mountainside and saw a heartening sight. Between a group of tents just below our own encampment, the summit of Mount Meru jutted up through a garland of sunlit clouds:

Mount Meru piercing up through the morning clouds. This is another active, but currently dormant, volcano. It last erupted in 1910

This is the mountain recommended for trekkers who have not had experience of relatively high-altitude trekking. It is reputedly an excellent preparatory climb before attempting Kilimanjaro. Alas, it also adds considerably to the overall cost of the expedition. In any event, I was now looking down at the summit of Mount Meru from a higher position on Kilimanjaro and congratulating myself on my progress so far. Not only that, but I was still not experiencing any appreciable effects of the altitude and started to feel optimistic about reaching the summit without too much difficulty. I should have reflected on the words of the prophet: 'pride cometh before a fall'. But that's another story to come!

Jon and I galloped over to the dining tent and loaded up our plates from the tempting array of breakfast foods. The rest of our group joined us, and the usual chatter gathered pace. The dining tent seemed hotter than usual, and I started to peel off first one layer of clothing and then another. This didn't help me very much, and I started to feel distinctly queasy.

I ran out of the tent and over to some tall clumps of heather just in time. There was no way I could go back into the dining tent after that. I just wanted to stay quietly in the cooler air. Jon and Patrick came over within a few moments to see how I was feeling. Patrick brought over a folding chair for me, and this was a good idea as my legs were feeling shaky. Jon offered to bring some food over to me, but the thought of eating anything just made me feel nauseous again. I felt sure that it was just the heat inside the dining tent that had upset my system, but I was aware that Patrick was looking sceptical about that idea. Patrick and our group leader, David, would now be watching my progress to determine whether or not I should be evacuated, especially in view of my age. It was up to me to get up to speed very quickly in order to remain with our group or be escorted back to Arusha. What promised to be an exciting day had turned into a struggle for survival if I was to get much farther up the mountain. I was on a challenge.

Our group set off amidst a wave of campsite-packing energy as the porters in the various other groups at Shira Camp zigzagged to and fro taking down tents, packing gear into manageable packs, and distributing the packs among themselves. It was dizzying.

I walked with Jon, and he agreed that Patrick had started to have doubts about how much higher I could reasonably be expected to climb. Jon knew that I still had plenty of energy in reserve to go higher. He also knew that my legs were strong, my breathing was good, and that I was the only one in our group of five who had not suffered from quite bad headaches from time to time in the past two days. I knew that my willpower was buoyant, the effects of altitude were no worse than anyone else's in our group, and that I felt confident and well enough to carry on. All I had to do now was to convince Patrick and David.

Patrick was a careful thinker with a lot of military experience dealing with a great variety of personnel in demanding situations. Dealing with civilians probably brought out a more protective and considerate side to him. Certainly, he didn't give the impression that he would want to drive us as he probably did his soldiers as an army major. I just had to impress this guy, or my party would be over.

We were about an hour into a steep but steady climb when Patrick walked alongside me and offered some advice on how to save energy by modifying the way I walked. He seemed to think that by carefully selecting how I negotiated where I chose to place my boots as we climbed up this steady gradient, I would save some energy. He pinpointed the fact that I didn't always take the easiest next step forward but sometimes stepped up onto a low rock rather than trying to step between two low-level adjacent rocks jutting into the narrow pathway. I took a gamble in the way I responded.

Firstly, I thanked Patrick for his helpful suggestion and agreed to give that way of walking more consideration in future. I knew that after years of backpacking, it would be difficult to alter my ingrained pattern of walking. I went on to say that the training I did in our gym back home emphasised leg strengthening exercises, including step-up routines using exercise steps. I suggested that stepping up onto raised levels every so often, instead of trying to find the lowest, easiest route on a pathway, was probably derived from the step-up routines that formed an important part of my fitness programme. Basically, I found it just such a natural thing to do, to break up what could otherwise become monotonous after a few hours of walking. I gradually veered the conversation over to the benefits I gained from my leg-strengthening training specifically designed for this trek up Kilimanjaro. The fact that I had not suffered any joint or muscle pains or soreness so far led me to think that I was in a 'go for it' condition and ready for what lay ahead of us. My energy level was high.

Patrick was clearly mulling over what I had been saying. He repeated that I needed to speak to him or David if I felt that this trek was too demanding for me or if I felt at all unwell. I assured him that as far as I was concerned, my nausea at breakfast was purely to do with the heat in the dining tent and that I had too many layers of clothing on. He seemed to be largely persuaded, but I knew that my every move was probably still being closely watched. Jon smirked as Patrick went over to talk with another member of our group.

"You may have just swung it, you silver-tongued devil."

I knew that Jon was pleased about us climbing together as high up this mountain as we could, but I re-emphasised to him that in the event of my being evacuated, he must carry on with the rest of the group. But Jon knew that my determination was now even stronger than when we first set foot on this mighty mountain. For the next hour or so, I mulled over in my mind just how much luck may be needed to supplement that determination.

We were approaching the Lava Tower. It was still about two miles away over some steep and rough terrain, but we were aiming to be there by lunchtime. The steep ascent gradually levelled, and the last section of the morning's trek was relatively flat.

Patrick came on the scene again and observed that my left leg was dragging. I explained that I banged my leg on a main pole of the dining tent at breakfast when I had to dash out to be ill away from our group as they were enjoying their meal. My leg wasn't badly injured, but I was favouring the right leg so far today in an effort to give the other leg a chance to get back to normal as the day wore on, and it was already feeling much better. As we talked, Patrick stared at my face. He called Jon over and asked him to look carefully at my face to assess whether it had slumped to one side and to tell him honestly if he thought that I had suffered a minor stroke.

I was speechless. Having felt increasingly strong and buoyant all morning after the passing nausea at breakfast, I just couldn't understand how Patrick came to this suspicion. Jon looked into my face. After a few moments of scrutiny, he said categorically to Patrick that I looked as I had always looked for the thirty-five years that he had known me, give or take the gradual and expected changes over that long period of time. He also put it forcefully to Patrick that he knew my capabilities well and had seen no reason to doubt my fitness for what lay ahead of us. This seemed to do the trick. Patrick gave me the benefit of the doubt.

We reached the Lava Tower shortly after that. The weather had suddenly changed as we clambered over the rocks to find somewhere to sit in relative comfort out of the increasing wind. The sky had become sullen, and it was time to put on warm clothing after a beautiful morning of sunshine. We were now at 4600 metres, and the effect of altitude had started to kick in.

I foraged for my packed lunch in my daypack. We were now in our third day, and the bread in the sandwiches was quite dry. Patrick came around to chat with the members of the group about the progress we had made so far. I could see that he spent more time looking in my direction than the other four in the group, and this probably signalled that he was still concerned about me.

After talking to the group, he came over to talk with me about how essential it was to keep drinking about four litres of water a day to counter the effects of altitude now that we were entering the zone where the oxygen level was becoming noticeably less. He then pointed out that I had not eaten any of my packed lunch. Not eating enough at this stage, when a lot more energy was needed to cope with the terrain in this alpine desert, could be just asking for trouble. I thought back to the time on the coastal footpath when the April blizzard slammed into Ian and me. Our hunger and near exhaustion then demanded all our remaining strength. The difference here was the altitude effect, and Patrick had a lot of experience in dealing with this testing dimension. I tried to eat the dry sandwich, but it was a struggle. Patrick was called away by our group leader, so rather than take the risk of upsetting my stomach again, I tossed the food into some adjacent rocks where two white-throated ravens were waiting to be fed. Clearly, they had tapped into various trekking groups' generosity over the years and knew how to play to the gallery for lunch surpluses. The sandwich disappeared in highly competitive seconds.

The weather had changed from morning sunshine to lunchtime clouds and chill, but as we set off for our first downhill section of the trek so far, the sun came out again to revive and warm us. The ravens cawed their good riddance to us in the rasping derision they seem to specialise in, but I just had to smile at their sheer brazenness.

David, our group leader, told us that Barranco Camp was straight ahead down the steep descent into the valley. We would be dropping down about 650 metres. By sleeping at a lower level than the 4600 metres we had climbed to today, acclimatisation should be speeded up, and we would be better prepared for the rigours of the following two days as we gradually ascended from 3950 metres to 5895 metres at the distant summit.

Our assistant guide, Filex, invited Jon and me to walk with him down into the valley at any pace we chose. I looked at Jon, and he understood immediately that I wanted to zip away at a fast pace to assure Patrick and David that my health was good and my energy level high. And this is exactly what we did.

Filex also seemed to understand what was in my mind, and he led us down into the valley at a galloping pace. I looked behind at one point, and we were well ahead of the main party. The mellow weather made me feel full of bounce, and Filex, Jon and I bounded like mountain goats down the easy path until we eventually reached the outer zone of the camp. Three of the younger members of the support team ran over to greet me joyously, almost as if they knew I had come through a test in a way that assured me of at least a chance at the summit. They were on 'Babu's' side, but whether they had placed bets on me getting to the summit base camp, or to the summit itself, I will never know. What I did know was that when Patrick and David arrived a little later, their concerns for me had diminished noticeably. I thanked my lucky stars that the way ahead for me, for at least the following day, looked good. Jon also was delighted with this outcome, and he gave me one of his closely guarded chocolate bars to celebrate, an act of startling generosity I will never forget. Surely, this was a memorable day!

On the way over to our tent, we looked across the valley to the Barranco Wall, our challenge for the following day. It loomed up steeply to nudge into the sky, and the near-vertical rock face was splintering the strong light into glittering facets that could have been intimidating to all but experienced mountaineers. Luckily, our route for the following day was mainly up a long, diagonal path with some exposed ledges thrown in for extra excitement, and not up the sheer rock face. Having said that, there was a warning written in the expedition brochure that it would be preferable if each member of the group had a head for heights. I recalled reading about this wall of rock elsewhere, and it seemed that more accidents and deaths have happened on this scramble than anywhere else on Kilimanjaro. I speculated that this could be in periods of wet weather when the soles of trekking boots didn't always have the same grip on the smooth, wet rock as in dry conditions. In any event, we were here now, and we would have to face whatever came our way on the following day.

The meal that evening was a joy for me as I had not eaten anything all day, except for the chocolate bar from Jon that had given me a sugar rush of epic proportions. I sensed that all five of us in our group were buoyant but also tense about what it would be like the next morning on the climb up the Barranco Wall. David and Patrick came in to speak with us after the meal. They tried to dispel any nervousness about the following day's climb up the Barranco, and it apparently had a steadying effect on all of us. Its reputation is well deserved, but by following the guidance of the leaders, we would be in good and highly experienced hands. On that note, we all went cheerfully to our tents on the chilliest night so far on the trip. I slept fairly well, but the thought of what the next day would bring circled fitfully around my mind.

TWENTY-ONE

The new day broke with the usual 'washy, washy' from one of the lads who passed in our bowls of hot water and fluffy flannels. Mugs of tea got us up and going to greet this day of scrambling up that fascinating, yet nerve-testing, rock face. I looked out of the tent flap to get a view of the monster as it effortlessly soared up through the thinning atmosphere into the blue world above. Could we really do this? Many others had faced their fears and climbed up this solidified lava wave that must have poured over from the summit of this mountain and then curtained down nearly two thousand metres into the Barranco Valley. I felt optimistic, and I detected that Jon was buzzing with unstoppable energy, ready to test himself on this particularly massive obstacle standing between us and the long haul up to the summit. If all went well, we would be leaving from the summit camp at midnight today to face what many climbers had found to be a test of strength and a spirit-crushing experience on the final eight hours of the ascent. Heaven help us!

The dining tent was also buzzing with anticipation from the rest of our group as we all dived into a welcome breakfast. Lunch would be in this same dining tent later in the day at a site overlooking the Karanga Valley, but we had the scrambling challenge and considerable trekking to do before reaching that point. I thought about our porters having to carry everything up the Barranco Wall, and then across the alpine desert before reaching Karanga camp. Once there, they had to set up the dining tent and help the cooks to get the meal under way before our main party arrived.

Many of the porters are not well equipped with mountain clothing, adequate sleeping bags, or even good boots for the job. They got by and always seemed happy and philosophical about their lot in life. I got the impression that they were among the fortunate ones in having this sort of work to do compared with many of their countrymen and women.

With breakfast over, we bustled out of the dining tent to collect our daypacks and water bottles. Straight across from us was the rock face, and we could pick out a group that had left before us, and they were just starting to claw their way over the steeply ascending rock ledges. It was difficult to tell from our distance away just how difficult they were finding it to scramble up that petrified lava 'waterfall'. But we would find out for ourselves very shortly.

We followed our guides down to the shallow river at the base of the wall. Crossing the river was no trouble, but we then almost immediately found ourselves on the diagonal pathway as it cut across the rock face. The vertical wall soaring up on our left would not have been possible for most people to climb. It would probably have been a challenge to even experienced mountaineers. Our route, although not easy even at this early stage of the climb, was at least viable. The pathway took some twists and turns at this point, and some of the rock steps required leg-stretching beyond what I had anticipated.

I looked down towards the Barranco Camp where the support team had already struck most of our camp. We had gained a surprising height in the first ten minutes of our climb, but it was still not a problem to the balance when looking down; that would come later! That thought suddenly brought an unwelcome memory back to me from my reading. Balance can become more of an issue as one enters old age. I just hoped that this wouldn't affect me too much when we had to negotiate the more exposed sections as we climbed higher. I had seen some of these sections on YouTube videos and heard some of the comments from some climbers who found them daunting.

Right on cue, just as I was thinking about this, a young lady in tears was being escorted back down to Barranco Camp by an assistant guide. The young lady was from the group ahead of ours and had apparently hit some problems. We found out later that she didn't have a head for heights, and even though her guides did their best to get her around a huge boulder that thrust out from the pathway, the drop below was just too much for her. The traverse involved a tricky placing of the feet and hands while edging around this cruel obstacle, and she was unable to move beyond the first foot and handholds. I heard one or two other trekkers ahead of me saying that they felt very nervous about some of the voids opening up below them and would be glad when we all reached the top of this climb.

Our group was nearing 'boulder hell', but first there came a fairly high and almost vertical rock step to scramble up. David and Patrick were already standing at the top of this step to help us individually scale this obstacle. I think Jon might have been further back, talking to one of the other members of our group. "Go for it," I said to myself, and before I realised it, my feet and hands found the perfect positions to lever myself up and over the edge of the step without assistance. David and Patrick looked impressed as they were kneeling at the top of the step ready to give assistance by hauling people up the last few feet. I knew that luck was with me, in addition to all the arm and leg strength training at the gym, but how would I fare with the boulder that I could just see coming into view?

David and Patrick waited until all five of us in the group had scrambled to the top of the step and then led the way to the boulder. They chatted to us about the looming obstacle and did their best to put us at ease. The good news was that this boulder presented us with the last substantial hurdle of the difficult section of this rock face. After that, we had less than an hour's steep ascent over relatively straightforward terrain to come to terms with, but the glorious views on this superb day would make it all worthwhile.

And there it was. The boulder shouldered its profound presence right across the narrow track and out over a big drop. It wasn't viable to try to climb over it because of the extra danger that presented. No, getting around the outer, exposed face of this thing with its little ripples of rocky surface was our way ahead. There were one or two small toeholds visible, but the trick was to start the traverse with the correct positioning of the hand and foot holds, otherwise halfway around the boulder, it would be extremely tricky to try to bring one leg through between the rock and one's other leg. David's experience would guide us individually as he directed and sequenced each move of hand and foot.

I was the second one to stretch out over the fearsome drop below, and I actually found it exciting in a perverse way. David called out each move as it was needed, and I rounded the boulder quite smoothly, reaching the other side in one piece with my heart pounding away like a steam hammer on steroids.

Each member of our group clambered around the rock successfully, and on we trekked up the remaining section of the wall in good spirits. The sun struck down now in an overfriendly way, and I thought about our porters forging ahead with all the heavy gear, contending with this heat. We didn't see them negotiating the boulder, but it clearly would have been their biggest challenge on the trek so far. I was full of admiration for them, and they really deserved the recommended bonuses we were going to give them on the last day of the expedition.

This Barranco Wall is stunning. It is a pity that two of the most-used routes up this mountain climb are further over to the east and don't come close to this exhilarating feature of the ascent. Our groups on the Lemosho route, who joined us near the Lava Tower, also climbed the Barranco, so it can become rather busy at times in view of the inevitable tailbacks while waiting for climbers in front to negotiate the various scrambling challenges.

All of a sudden, we were at the top of the wall. There was a vast vista stretching out over the countryside a long way below us, and we could take all of this in while we stopped for a rest and photo opportunities. Everyone was in fine spirits as we enjoyed the twenty minutes' rest in the sun. I took a moody shot of Jon with the huge bulwark of the mountain's summit rearing up behind him. He looked like a real mountaineer with his beard and well-chosen clothing for this climb:

Jon below part of the following day's daunting final ascent to the summit

*Two of our wonderful porters reaching the top
of the Barranco Wall after a heroic effort*

Our group. I am on the left of the shot next to our great expedition leader, David

I thought that this could be the picture to get enlarged and framed as a memento when we eventually got back home again, although that seemed a long way away at that moment. That thought coaxed me to think about what Judith and Jon's mother Vivien were getting up to on the Isles of Scilly, a few miles off Cornwall's Land's End, where they had gone on holiday. I had never been there but, given good weather, it would be glorious at this time of year.

My reverie was interrupted by the assistant guides rounding us all up to get ready to set off on the next leg of the journey towards Karanga Valley, but not before we took a group photo:

We were about to head off into the alpine desert, the penultimate zone before the attempt on the even more rugged terrain of the summit zone later that day. The top of the Barranco Wall phased quickly into this desert world, and the ground became sandy and hot. We marched down a long path onto a plateau interspersed with its valleys and creases in the ground that would have made it hard going even for tanks. The guides pointed out the area we were heading for in the far distance on a ridge the other side of this wide and torrid Karanga Valley. We had great views of the spectacular southern rim of the ice fields, but it was becoming so hot underfoot that one could easily imagine that the magma seething not that far below us was in league with the sun to determine how to test our resolve to make progress towards our lunch stop. This surely was the 'sun's anvil'.

We eventually approached the base of the ridge. It was at this point that we crossed a narrow river, and this was the last opportunity to collect water before the attempt on the summit at midnight. Our porters had overtaken us on the Barranco Wall and had already refilled our camp's water containers ready for the evening meal and also the following day's trek down to the final camp. But first of all, we would need water for the long afternoon's trek up to Barafu Camp, the last camp before the climb up to the summit during the long, dark hours of the night.

Drinking the required amount of water had become a problem for me and some of the others in our group. I had tried desperately to drink the recommended four litres a day in an effort to minimise the increasing effects of altitude as we climbed higher. This had been a challenge during the whole trek so far, but now it had become a loathsome penance. What had changed? I had not thought about it before the ascent, but water boils more quickly as the air pressure decreases. That may seem to be an advantage, but it doesn't work that way. In common with many sources of water, microorganisms and various bacteria can enter the water, and some of them are not good for human consumption. This is why it was often good practice to boil all drinking water on this mountain to make it safe to drink. Another method was to filter the water through an effective strainer with micromesh or a type of carbon granule filter, but the problem there was that the water for each day's trek was boiled up during breakfast and passed to us in our very hot drinking flasks. It was not practical to try to decant this while en route. This then meant that we were strongly advised to use some extra method of purification, usually tablets that I found to be utterly distasteful and so repellent that the water made me feel ill. The inevitable result was that the four- to five-litre intake of water per day to help ward off some of the effects of the altitude was not achieved; as a consequence, events later that day caught me out.

We are apparently on the brink of a breakthrough with water purification when travelling in wild country. The wonderful new material, graphene, is being developed on an industrial scale for water treatment, and it is apparently planned to bring this super-efficient filtration material into small-scale use, such as in backpacking. Not only is it such a fine filter that water taken from most usual sources will be rendered pure for drinking, but it seems that it will also make sea water drinkable by filtering out virtually everything that isn't found in our everyday drinking water. I imagine that the cost of this new technology will be steep, at least in the early stages.

We left the little river to flow and sing over the lava stones in its weedy channel and started to climb the steep slope leading up to the top of the ridge where, from all accounts, lunch would be waiting for us. I followed Filex, one of our assistant guides, as he kept the pace down to a reasonable level. The altitude effect came upon me quite quickly. Filex spotted this quickly and signalled for our group to rest for a minute or two. My breathing recovered its rhythm within about a minute, and Filex assured me that at four thousand metres, this was to be generally expected in most parties that he had escorted. One or two others in our group had also felt the increasing effects of the altitude.

We pressed on. I asked for another quick rest before we reached the dining tent further up the ridge, and again I only needed a minute or two before being ready to get back into the climb. Jon encouraged me all the way up the ridge and kindly offered to carry my pack. This wasn't needed, but I did appreciate the offer.

The dining tent came into view, and the lads gave us a warm welcome as soon as they spotted us. They really were a great pleasure to be with. The lunch was served up straight away, and it was remarkable how they had carried all the tents and cooking gear up the Barranco Wall, over the plateau, up to the ridge, and then prepared a good meal for us with perfect timing.

There was time for a short rest after the lunch before setting out for Barafu Camp at 4600 metres. As we chatted about the long haul of the morning, the light in the dining tent began to change. It had become darker. I looked outside and saw that a mist had rolled in. The visibility had been reduced to just a few metres, and I was thankful that we had reliable and experienced guides to take us up the next section of the increasingly rugged alpine desert through the unnerving curtain of thick mist.

We grabbed our gear and assembled outside the tent with the guides. Into the mist we went, huddling close together to make sure that no one became lost. Low and behold, the mist quickly cleared, and we were back into a sultry and heat-rippling afternoon. Mountains certainly know how to surprise trekkers and climbers taking a chance on the weather as they journey up through the different altitudes.

My breathing had become normal again, and I started to wonder about what the night ascent to the summit would bring in the way of challenges and surprises. We trekked onwards and upwards through the hot afternoon with the huge bulk of the summit's main volcanic cone glaring down at us on our left. I had not experienced any muscle or joint problems at all on the trip so far. Most of the accounts I had read about climbing this mountain brought in the problem about aching limbs and a general feeling that exhaustion was creeping up remorselessly on the writers long before reaching the point we had now reached. If only I could cope with the altitude, I felt that the summit would be feasible for me. But to be on the safe side, I emphasised again to Jon that in the event of my not being able to make it, he had to carry on with the rest of the group. A guide would be assigned to take me back to Barafu Camp, where I would wait for the group to return, exhausted but exhilarated from their summit experience. Jon assured me that he would want me to carry on if the altitude got the better of him. We had agreed on this pact, and that set my mind more at ease.

The afternoon heat tried to barbeque us, but with the sun-blocker, the wide-brimmed hats, and the very slow and measured pace set by our guide, we just about managed to make reasonable progress towards Barafu Camp. We hadn't spotted the camp yet, but with a decided up-tilt in the ground, we knew that we were on the steepening side of the Kibo crater where the camp was situated.

The altitude had started to hit me by this time, and I needed to ask our guide, Filex, to rest for a minute or two. He asked me to keep just behind him as we set off again, and I noticed that our group, David, and Patrick were spaced out in a column behind us. There was very little being said as we trekked on, as everyone did their best to conserve energy. The climb became steeper and more demanding. I needed to catch my breath by stopping just for a minute every few hundred yards. I didn't want to cause a nuisance to the rest of our people, so I kept my rest breaks to a minimum. Jon told me later that the others were impressed by my maximum effort to keep going regardless of the merciless effect of the lack of oxygen at this altitude.

We were at about 4500 metres when Barafu Camp 'village' came into view. There were about fifteen tents, two large dining tents, and a tiny toilet hut perched high up on a grassy bank above the camp. We still needed to gain another hundred metres of steep climbing up the side of the volcanic cone before we could all relax over welcome mugs of tea or coffee. Plodding on was not easy, but at least we now had restored motivation in our upwards progress. I thought about our support team's effort in trekking up the same route but with much more weight to carry than we had. They also had to haul the extra weight of the water up from the river we crossed before the lunch break. These guys fully deserved the bonuses recommended by the travel company. They also merited our unstinting praise.

We reached the camp at the end of the afternoon, feeling well stretched and oxygen-deprived. Jon and I walked slowly up to the toilet hut from our tent, and even this brought home the true extent of the oxygen deprivation. The effect on me probably wasn't helped by my utter revulsion at drinking any more than a few sips an hour of the medicated water. My physical fitness level seemed to be all right; it was just the effect of the altitude that oppressed me. It had been a hot and gruelling trek that day, and after the evening meal, we would only be able to get three hours' sleep at the most before attempting to get through one of the most punishing nights of our lives as the first part of tomorrow's eighteen-hour day before arriving at the final camp way down the mountain on the Mweka Route.

The call for tea and biscuits was welcome. In the chatter of the dining tent, I soon forgot about feeling sorry for myself. It seemed that everyone in the group had felt the strain today, and it was generally felt that one extra day of acclimatisation on this Machame Route would have made all the difference. Nevertheless, we were all quite optimistic about being able to at least attempt the summit climb at midnight.

There was about an hour or so before the evening meal would be ready, but we all lingered in the dining tent to chatter and compare notes about the trip so far. After a while, Jon and I went back to our tent for a sort-out of the gear for the night's long and very steep climb. We had almost finished the preparations when we heard the call for the evening meal.

Jon went ahead while I lingered to look eastwards. I climbed up a nearby ridge, and there it was: the secondary volcanic cone, Mawenzi, 5149 metres. I mentioned much earlier in this story that a deeply sad event occurred on that huge cone. A close friend of mine told me what happened.

In the 1950s, his brother was the radio officer aboard a *Douglas Dakota* aircraft. On that day, there were about twenty-two passengers and crew on board for an internal flight in Africa.

The aircraft was in the vicinity of Kilimanjaro when a huge storm erupted, darkening the sky to the point where visual navigation was impossible. It seems that the electrical storm also affected many of the plane's instruments, and this made the situation desperate. The aircraft crashed into Mawenzi, killing everyone on board.

My friend, Mike Gregory, asked me before I set out on this trekking expedition if I would say a few words from him to his brother, Arthur Percy Gregory, when I was in the vicinity of the site of the crash. This was the perfect moment, with the glowing twilight sending out its other-worldly tranquillity over the world around me. It was a moving moment that I will never forget as I spoke the words that Mike wanted me to convey. My own struggles with the altitude were now firmly put into perspective.

I clambered slowly over the stony ground to reach the dining tent. The group had assembled, and the meal was just being served. It was a quite jolly mealtime, but one could sense the underlying preoccupation with what lay ahead for us in just a few hours' time after our rest back in the tents. David went over the important points about the night climb up to the summit, and then we dispersed for a final check of the essential gear and to get some rest before the call at 11.30pm. It seems that there were to be hot drinks and biscuits arranged for us all before the zero-hour at midnight.

Jon and I walked down to our tent just as the night wind started to flap everything around us on the campsite. That wind had an icy edge to it, and we agreed that our investment in the quality mountain jackets – which we had not needed so far – was a great idea.

Jon clambered into his sleeping bag and, unusually for him, seemed to fall asleep quickly. I sat on my sleeping bag, leaned forwards to unlace my boots, and hit a wall. The altitude effect slammed into me. My breathing became not just laboured but difficult in an alarming way. I sat back again, and this helped to make my breathing a little easier. After resting in that position for a while, I felt well enough to put a new set of batteries into my head torch ready for the trek up into the darkness towards the eventual summit. I tried and tried again to get the new batteries into the torch but my coordination was worryingly lacking.

Jon's breathing convinced me that he was sleeping soundly, and I didn't want to wake him. I reached into my clothing bag and found enough warm garments to pull over me as I lay on the sleeping bag, and sleep came upon me quickly. That sleep lasted about two hours, and then I suddenly jolted myself awake by suffering violent shivering right through my body. There was a bitingly cold blast of air right against my back, and I knew that hypothermia was imminent. Stretching out my arm towards the inner door of the tent, it became obvious that I had not fully joined up the double zips, and the wind that was shaking the tent had forced its way into the inner tent where I had unknowingly become a draught excluder. I was in a bad way.

Jon surfaced at this point and rapidly assessed my condition. This greatly concerned him, and he helped me into my sleeping bag to get my core warmed up in order to fend off the full effects of hypothermia. He was just about to go to Patrick's tent for assistance when Patrick came down the slope to our tent to tell us that it was time to go up to the dining tent for a hot drink. I could hardly speak because of my violent shivering, but Jon explained the situation to him and said that he didn't feel too well himself, and he would stay with me to make sure that I would be all right. Patrick's disappointment was obvious. I urged Jon to go on the summit trek, but he insisted on staying with me. I burrowed down into my warm sleeping bag and soon started to feel the benefit of it. Sleep overtook me quickly in my exhausted state.

* * *

I woke up suddenly about half an hour after midnight, and something in my mind beckoned me to leave the tent. I was still breathless with the reduced oxygen available to my lungs, but I knew that whatever was exerting this power over me needed to be pursued. Crawling quietly out of the tent in order not to disturb Jon, I noticed immediately that the furious wind had dropped away. A penetrating, sharp coldness had taken its place.

I stood up to stretch, and as I looked upwards towards the night sky, the most amazing sight greeted me. A dazzling, crystal-clear view of the heavens, such as I had never seen before, made me catch what remained of my breath. The celestial beauty and power overwhelmed my senses, and my breathing became rapid, shallow, and frightening.

My breathing thankfully began to settle back quickly into a more familiar struggle with the lack of oxygen at this height, but the night sky continued to transfix me. Myriads of stars sequinned their tiny beams across the blackness of space, and great galaxies seemed like glowing fingerprints spaced out against this glittering 'stardust' that filled the night sky. But most striking of all was our Milky Way Galaxy with its billions of stars like our sun. It is so vast that it takes about 240 million years for our solar system to rotate around the galaxy's centre. Our own solar system is about twenty-five thousand light years from the centre of the Milky Way, and yet our galaxy is just one of a colossal number. The macro scale of all this is awesome. But to me, a staggering fact is that we as human beings in the micro end of the cosmos are apparently the most complex single entities in the known universe.

Seneca, a Stoic philosopher in Ancient Rome, was so profoundly impressed by the heavens, he ventured to speculate that if the whole of philosophy in its unity were to be spread out in the great firmament like the stars, then philosophy would ravish all mortals with love for her.

The Chinese philosopher, Lao Tzu (sixth century BCE) said that: 'to the mind that is still, the whole universe surrenders', and I felt strongly that some part of the universe had penetrated into my being that wonderful night. Not only that, but it felt as if I was destined to be there. From the time when Jon persuaded me to join him on the expedition to Kilimanjaro, I had a vague feeling that destiny had played a part in my decision.

Perhaps contemplating the night sky on such a night, in all its glorious beauty and mystery, is the nearest we can get to the deepest level of mindfulness, within 'feeling distance' of the very heart of things. The Neoplatonist, Plotinus, believed that the highest level of awareness is incommunicable by the intellect; it is an upwards journey of the soul.

My thoughts returned to Hofmannsthal and his belief that we find ourselves, and reality, in those moments of our deepest enchantment. This night, near the summit of Kilimanjaro, under the enormity of the universe in its crystalline array, took me to a place of such deep enchantment that I felt completely at one with myself.

I was held, statue-like, by the sheer joy of this moment, but I could feel the icy cold of this high place seeping into my already-weakened body. The tears of exhilaration were freezing onto my face. It was time to go back to the tent, snuggle into my sleeping bag, fall into a deep sleep, and be ready for the new day; the first day of the rest of my life.

My mountain journey was over. My new journey into a changed life was about to begin.

AFTERWORD

Do I still sip from the fountain of youth and adventure? Well, I am planning to solo-backpack two hundred miles along the South West Coast Path next year (2022) to celebrate entering my eightieth year. Clearly, I haven't learnt my lesson yet, but at least there will be more than twice the amount of oxygen to breath at sea level than near the top of Kilimanjaro.

Can people of any age, and in good health, safely drink from the fountain of youth and adventure? It's worth considering. It may keep you young in mind and body way beyond your average expectations.

This book is printed on paper from sustainable sources managed under the Forest Stewardship Council (FSC) scheme.

It has been printed in the UK to reduce transportation miles and their impact upon the environment.

For every new title that Matador publishes, we plant a tree to offset CO_2, partnering with the More Trees scheme.

MORE TREES
LET'S PLANT A BILLION TREES

For more about how Matador offsets its environmental impact, see www.troubador.co.uk/about/